DOPAMINE DRESSMAKING

To my wee man,
Your sweet dreams
helped me find
the dopamine
in dressmaking.
This book is for you.

Brogan Allard

DOPAMINE DRESSMAKING

15 Sewing Patterns For Every Season

Photography by Olivia Bossert & Elliya Cleveley
Illustrations by Robin Blair

quadrille

The T-shirt Dress
The Sun Dress
The Tea Dress
The Buffet Dress

The Everyday Dress

The Bib Dress

The Shirt Dress

The Party Dress

INTRODUCTION

Well, hello there!

I can't tell you how happy I am that you're here. Fashion lovers, budding dressmakers, seasoned seamstresses… Whoever you are, this book is for you.

We may not have met before, so in that case, let me introduce myself. I'm Brogan, a 27-year-old dressmaker and social-media content creator. I live in Leicestershire with my husband, baby boy and sausage dog, and I'm well and truly addicted to dresses. After featuring as a Finalist on Series 8 of *The Great British Sewing Bee*, I've become known for my ultra-feminine, romantic style, and I'm on a mission to inspire a new generation of stylish sewers.

From a young age I always loved to be creative. However, my passion for sewing didn't come along until a little later, when I was bought my first sewing machine at 15 years old. In true 'Brogan-style', I had to get started immediately and I took to YouTube to learn the basics. My first garment was a tweed cape, complete with sparkly love-heart buttons. Looking back, it was really quite hideous, but I was filled with pride when I strolled into school wearing my one-of-a-kind outerwear. From that moment on, I was hooked. Through lots of trial and error (and more ill-fitting garments than I'd care to admit), I developed my skills and now have my dream wardrobe filled with all my favourite things: puff sleeves, gingham and frills.

However, throughout my sewing journey, I found it hard to find designs that fully embody my personal style, and I would spend hours mixing and matching different patterns to create the perfect garment – not an easy process for an inexperienced sewer! From these experiences, the idea behind *Dopamine Dressmaking* was born: a book to inspire new sewers, help others to make one-of-a-kind garments and, above all, show that it's so darnn cool to sew.

DOPAMINE DRESSING

Arguably one of the most talked-about trends from recent years, catwalk shots and street-style images of dopamine dressing fill our social feeds in 2024, and for good reason! Unsure how to channel a dopamine vibe in your own outfits? Let's talk about it!

Simply put, it's dressing for joy. You can do this by reaching for garments in your wardrobe that bring a smile to your face, or pairing bright colours that literally brighten up the streets you walk down. It's feel-good fashion at it's finest and regardless of your age, your style or where you live, you can bring some extra dopamine to your day through your fashion choices.

In high school, I was desperate to fit in. I also had a lot of passions outside of school: most of my time was spent in dance or musical theatre clubs, or sat in front of my sewing machine. This didn't leave much time to socialize and often left me feeling like a bit of an outsider. No one else made their clothes or spent their weekends in fabric shops, and they certainly didn't appreciate how much time went into adding embroidery to a cardigan or beading your own trainers! I often felt that if I went out and bought that on-trend bag that all the 'cool girls' were wearing, then I might fit in a little more.

It took a good few years, but as my dressmaking skills grew, so did my appreciation of my own abilities. I soon realized that the coolest thing you can wear is confidence, and if you're truly happy in yourself, it shines out to others from within. No fashion trend can mimic that inner beauty. From that moment on, I truly understood the meaning of dopamine dressing, long before it featured in spreads in fashion magazines. Choosing outfits that are unapologetically you can brighten your mood, and tell people a little bit about you as soon as you step into a room. So if you want to bring a little bit of joy to your wardrobe, dopamine dressing is for you!

I want to emphasize that dopamine dressing is about what makes you happy – there are definitely no rule books! But if you're looking for some suggestions of where to start, here are my favourite ways to spark some joy:

Play with colour

Unexpected colour pairings are my favourite fashion statement! Think of a contrasting combo you enjoy like pink and green, or maybe orange and a vibrant purple, and build an outfit focusing solely on these colours. You'd be surprised at the combinations you can create with things you already have in your wardrobe.

If you're feeling less bold, you can try colour blocking. Pick your favourite colour (mine is pink, always!) and try to dress only in that colour. You can experiment with different tones, shades and textures to create a really fun outfit. Take a look at my Buffet Dress styling on pages 184–185 to see some blue colour blocking in action.

Pattern clash

My favourite way to bring some sunshine to my wardrobe is to pattern clash: find two prints that you love and pair them together! Again, there are no hard-and-fast rules on what you can and can't do, but I like to find a common colour thread within the prints to help the outfit gel together. A great example is my Tea Dress on page 66.

Accessory overload

Feeling like going all-out with your outfit? Go wild with your accessories! We're talking hair clips, statement earrings, frilly socks and statement shoes. Accessories can add so much fun to a basic outfit so don't be afraid to push your own boundaries. Check out my hair look on page 118 for the ultimate rainbow hair inspiration!

If it brings a smile to your face when wearing it, it's dopamine dressing. So let go of those boring fashion rules and be your own trendsetter!

WHAT'S IN MY SEWING KIT

A good sewing kit can take years to perfect, and it can sometimes feel overwhelming shopping for haberdashery when there are so many options to choose from. Don't worry if you're just starting out, as I've compiled a list of all my sewing essentials, so you don't have to!

Sewing machine

One of the most frequently asked questions on my socials is what sewing machine I would recommend for a beginner. Often people mistakenly assume that you need a high-tech machine to be able to sew your own garments, which is far from the truth. Most basic sewing machines offer a variety of stitches and the ability to sew a buttonhole, which are the essentials for getting started. I would always recommend first opting for a cheaper machine to learn the basics on, before upgrading further down the line.

Overlocker/serger

For the more avid sewers amongst you, I would highly recommend investing in an overlocker. It really is a game changer for making your garments look better and last longer. However, I made it through nine years of sewing before I got one, so it's definitely not a necessity. Feel free to use other methods to finish your raw edges, such as zigzag stitch or even French seams.

Iron & ironing board

These are essential for preparing fabric and pressing our seams as we sew. It's best if your iron has the function to choose the level of heat and steam based on the type of fabric you are using.

Scissors/rotary cutter

Many of the sewers I know are scissor snobs, and for good reason! Good scissors can make all the difference when it comes to cutting out fabric accurately. I always recommend the Milward extra-sharp range: they've been a firm favourite of mine for years now. I like to have a smaller pair of thread scissors or snips to hand too.

I have also more recently discovered the pleasure of using a rotary cutter, which can make cutting out even quicker and more efficient. This will cut through a regular table surface, so it needs to be teamed with a cutting mat. It's a great option if you have space for a large cutting mat (or two) in your sewing area.

Thread

Another sewing item that can spark controversy is thread. Some sewers swear by more expensive brands, however, I have had positive experiences with all types of price points. Coats Moon thread has always worked for me and is a great price, although I do now like to invest in Güttermann as it has a fantastic range of colours and the threads run smoothly through my machine. Regardless of the brand, start out with your basic colours and you can build up your stash as and when needed.

Dressmaking pins

These little devils seem to get lost in all the crevices of my sewing room. They get bent, blunted and, more often than not, sucked up the hoover... so it's safe to say you'll need a lot. They are essential when it comes to securing fabric in place ready to sew and are a lot easier to keep track of with a magnetic pin dish.

PFAFF
passport 3.0

Safety pins

You might think these are old-fashioned, but one of these makes all the difference when you're trying to thread elastic through a casing. Pin it on to the end of the elastic, close it up and start threading – you can feel the safety pin through the fabric as you ease it along.

Tool for fabric marking

Tailor's chalk would be the traditional choice, but personally I prefer to use a fabric pen to transfer any necessary pattern markings to my fabric. A recent discovery for me has been the Pilot Frixion pen, which easily removes with heat, but there's a whole range of water-soluble markers on the market too.

Sewing-machine needles

It's always a good idea to have a pack of spare machine needles to hand. Your needle will need to be changed regularly to ensure it is sharp and to keep your machine running smoothly. I like to have a pack of Universal needles for my woven fabrics and some ballpoint needles for my stretch fabrics. You will see that most packs come with a range of sizes: size 70/10 needles are best for thinner fabrics, and heavier fabrics such as denim or twill need a larger size 90/14 needle.

Loop turner

One extra sewing tool that I cannot live without is my Prym Turning Set. If you're fed up of spending too long trying to turn out thin straps or waist ties, you need this in your life. You choose a tube and stick depending on the width of your strap or tie and then use both items to turn your strap out in a matter of seconds. Thank me later.

Top tip!

There are so many other sewing gadgets and goodies out there that you may like to try when you are further into your dressmaking journey, but this basic kit is pretty much all you could ever need.

FABRIC FOCUS

One of the most important choices you have to make before sewing up your garment is the fabric, and it's arguably one of the most fun parts too! The composition of a fabric can have a big impact on your final make, so it's a good idea to take plenty of time to choose the option right for you. First of all, think about where you intend wearing the dress. Is it meant to be something you can throw on to run errands? Or is it destined for a special occasion? Is it the kind of garment that will be getting washed regularly, or will it hang in pride of place in your wardrobe until your next party? Have a look at my fabric suggestions below to find your perfect fabric pairing.

Brocade (jacquard)

The perfect option for a statement garment like the Party Dress (see page 164). Traditionally made from silk (think *Bridgerton* vibes!), this fabric is generally now made from a mix of fibres through a process called 'jacquarding', which creates its signature embroidered look. Thanks to its weave, brocade has a distinct 'right' and 'wrong' side to the fabric, and you can choose to use either side – or both – giving you the opportunity to play around with the different textures and colours within the fabric. This is my go-to for show-stopping occasion wear.

Broderie Anglaise

One of my all-time favourites, this fabric is known for its signature eyelet cut-outs that create uniform patterns across it. It gives the same effect as lace but scaled up to be suitable for more casual garments such as blouses or dresses. This would be perfect for the Shirt Dress (see page 144).

Chambray

Lightweight and cotton based, this woven fabric can be used as an alternative to denim for summer garments. It's extremely versatile and is a great one to have in your stash for staple garments.

Cotton

One of the most popular materials in the world, cotton is a light and natural fabric that can be used for a variety of garments. It's a stable fabric that handles nicely and presses well, and I'd therefore recommend this as the perfect fabric for a beginner sewer.

Denim

A classic, hard-wearing fabric most popularly used for jeans and outerwear. The weight of this fabric will determine what garments it would be suitable for. A lightweight washed 112g (4oz) denim could be perfect for a shirt dress.

Double gauze

Made from two layers of fine cotton gauze, this super-breathable and comfy fabric is the perfect choice for summer. This would make the dreamiest Sun Dress (see page 48).

Jersey

This stretch fabric comes in a whole range of weights and designs. Mixed with viscose, it offers a beautiful drape alongside some stretch and could be a great option for the Everyday Dress (see page 104). More stable jerseys, like a single-knit cotton, are traditionally used in T-shirts and are therefore perfect for the T-shirt Dress (page 30).

Linen

Look in any RTW (ready-to-wear) clothing store right now and you'll find linen. Made from natural fibres, and with great eco credentials, this versatile fabric can be used for a whole host of garments. From shirts to dresses, it offers a beautiful drape and can keep you cool in summer. It does have a tendency to crease easily but can look stunning in solid colours.

Satin/duchess satin

Another fantastic option for those dressier makes, satin is known for its lustrous finish and is a popular choice for evening wear. Duchess satin features a high thread count. It therefore holds its shape well and can make an incredible puff sleeve, making it an ideal pairing for the Party Dress (see page 164).

Taffeta

Taffeta is a crisp, lightweight fabric that often has an incredible shine to it and usually comes in a wide variety of eye-catching colours. For less experienced sewers, this would make a great option for occasion wear as it's a fairly stable fabric to cut out and sew.

Viscose/crêpe

This has to be my most-used fabric type in my handmade wardrobe and for good reason! Viscose is a lightweight and drapey fabric made from cellulose (from plant fibres such as wood pulp), that is relatively affordable but soft to wear. Viscose comes in a wide variety of designs and is often blended with other fibres such as linen. It can be more slippery to work with than cotton, but would be a great fabric to move on to as your confidence in dressmaking grows.

FABRIC SHOPPING & SUSTAINABILITY

Sustainability is becoming a big talking point in the sewing community, and rightly so! The fashion industry is responsible for an ever-growing amount of garment and fabric waste, which has drastic environmental effects. Buying less and sewing your own clothes is a great way to reduce your carbon footprint, but even buying fabrics can have its disadvantages. Here are some of my top tips to keep your sewing journey as sustainable as possible.

Take time to plan

I'm sure we can all agree that buying a top from a fast-fashion brand and throwing it away a few months later isn't a good choice for the environment, but over-producing handmade items can be just as bad. It can be tempting to try to keep up with the catwalks and sew new trend-led pieces each season, but chances are, these aren't going to be pieces you reach for in two years' time and they will ultimately add to our issue of garment waste. Try to analyze what you need in your wardrobe and plan your projects from there. Take into account fabrics and colours that would work well with pieces you already own. If you have an idea for a new make, think about how many outfit combinations you could create with it. I've included lots of styling advice in this book to help you make the most of your garments through all seasons.

Consider buying deadstock

I am a huge fan of deadstock fabrics. These are essentially surplus materials that are left over by fabric mills or factories. This can be for a few different reasons: the company bought more than it needed, it didn't work for the garment they wanted to produce, or there may be a small flaw in the material. There is an ever-growing market for these fabrics in the world of sewing. There are many specialist fabric shops that stock a wide range of these deadstocks that would otherwise go to landfill. Often, they come at bargain prices, and you can even pick up some ex-designer prints that you may recognize from the high street or past designer collections!

Check out preloved

When I was younger, it was definitely more taboo to openly talk about shopping second-hand. However, there's been a big change in recent years with platforms like Vinted combatting these stereotypes and making it cool to buy preloved. Some of my favourite purchases this year have been preloved and it's amazing what kind of materials you find in your local charity shops, so don't rule them out. I'm always on the hunt for vintage bedsheets and tablecloths as they are perfect for making dresses and can add a cool vintage vibe to a me-made garment.

Get to know your terminology

When fabric shopping it can be difficult to know what really is a sustainable option. Looking out for these key terms will help you make more informed purchasing decisions:

- **Oeko-Tex®:** Fabrics with this label have been carefully tested for harmful chemicals and none have been found throughout the manufacturing process.
- **GOTS certified:** This means that the fabric has proven to be sustainable according to a global standards agency that looks at all parts of the fabric's lifecycle from its raw materials to its manufacturing process and labelling.
- **Organic:** Fabrics certified to be organic have been produced in a way that doesn't use any harmful chemicals during the process, which means it is significantly better for the environment than non-organic options. It's still important to consider the type of organic fabric you are choosing, however. For example, the process of manufacturing cotton is still very water intensive. You may want to consider an option such as linen instead, which requires much less water to produce.
- **Recycled:** There are a whole host of fabrics now available that are produced from recycled materials, which means that no new resources have been used to make them, and fabric waste has therefore also been reduced. A great example of this is recycled polyester, which is generally made from plastic bottles that would otherwise go to landfill.
- **Lyocell/Tencel™:** This lightweight fabric is made from wood pulp and is 100% biodegradable, making it a sustainable fabric option. You may find it blended with other fibres, such as linen.

It's important to remember that it's very hard to be fully sustainable when buying new, and it's also pretty hard to be perfect! I think, as long as you are well-informed and making conscious purchases, you're doing your bit to sew sustainably.

THE SEWING DICTIONARY

I remember starting out on my sewing journey like it was yesterday, and one of the hardest parts was wrapping my head around 'pattern-speak'. With my younger self in mind, I've compiled a list of all the main sewing techniques we'll be using in the projects and explained them in the simplest terms possible. Also, make sure to check out my technique tutorials throughout the book, as some of the more complicated terms are explained in more detail there.

Baste (tack)

Basting is used to hold two pieces of fabric together before sewing the final seam and gives a firmer hold than just pinning. We do this by increasing our stitch length on our machine to its maximum and sewing a line of stitches. This can later be removed by unpicking the stitches if you need to.

Clip curves

When sewing around curves, it can be difficult for the fabric to lay fully flat once turned the right way out. To combat this, we make small cuts at right-angles to the seam allowance which go as close to the stitch line as possible without cutting into any stitches. This allows the fabric to move and lay flatter rather than bunching up.

Edgestitch

This is when we sew extremely close to an edge, usually about 0.2cm (⅛in) away, and this can be used to hold facings in place and improve the overall finish of the garment. It can also be used to close turning gaps.

Gather

Gathering is one of my favourite techniques, which will feature often throughout the projects. It reduces the width of a wide piece of fabric, whilst also creating fullness that can be used to make full skirts and puff sleeves. It is created by running long basting stitches across the fabric and pulling on the thread tails to bring it in (see my technique tutorial on page 64 for more on this).

Interfacing

This is a type of fabric that is used to make parts of a garment more stable. It comes in different weights and types (woven, non-woven, knitted, sew-in, iron-on...), but generally you should pick the weight that is closest to the kind of fabric you are using or slightly lighter. The most common type found in craft shops tends to be a cheaper, paper-like interfacing. I find this doesn't wash well or stand the test of time in garments. Where possible, I try to find fusible woven interfacing: this feels a lot more fabric-like and wrinkles less when ironed on.

Notches

Notches are pattern markings that help us attach pattern pieces to each other correctly and help us ensure that everything in our garment is lining up as it should. They are indicated with small lines on the edge of a pattern piece. Usually, single notches are used on front pattern pieces and double notches are used on the back ones. On a sleeve, there will be a single notch on the side that attaches to the front bodice and double notches where it attaches to the back bodice. Match double notches to double notches and single notches to single ones. When cutting out the pattern in your chosen fabric, use a small pair of scissors to cut along the lines in the pattern to mark each notch. It's an easy step to forget, but it makes all the difference when it comes to sewing up a garment.

Press

This is a dressmaker's term for ironing a part of your fabric. Generally, whenever we sew a seam, we will need to press it afterwards to ensure the fabric lays flat. It is always a good idea to do this as you go along throughout a project, rather than leaving it all to the end. It really does make a garment look more professional and can even affect the way a garment fits.

Seam allowance

This is one of the most commonly used terms you will find in a pattern, and it refers to the distance between the edge of the fabric and where you will sew a seam line. It can vary depending on what brand of pattern you are using, but generally in these projects we will be using a 1cm (⅜in) seam allowance. This means that you will need to line your fabric up with the 1cm (⅜in) marking on your sewing machine's plate when sewing your seam.

Shirring

This is an amazing technique to gather in fabric and can make stretchy and figure-hugging garments. When shirring, we swap out the regular thread on our bobbin for a specialist elastic thread that will give your stitches the iconic shirring stretch. Shirring does require specific sewing-machine settings alongside this (see page 122 for more details) and can be tricky to master on different machines. I promise though, once you find the correct settings for your machine, it works like a dream every time.

Stay stitch

Stay stitching is done with a short stitch length, usually along a curved edge, such as a neckline, to prevent stretching as we sew. It can be done as soon as you've cut out the piece and helps prevent fraying as well as stretching. This is usually stitched just within the seam allowance so it doesn't show on the outside of the finished garment. It's an easy step to miss but can make a huge difference to the overall fit and finish of your garment.

Understitch

This is when we sew the seam allowance to a facing or lining to prevent it from rolling forward and showing on the outside of a garment. It's one of those professional touches that can make all the difference to a neckline. See my technique tutorial on understitching on page 178.

PROJECT PREP

I hate to break it to you, but if you want to build your dream handmade wardrobe, there's a whole lot of preparation that needs to go into a project before we can even think of turning on our machine. Something I've learned over my 10 years of sewing is that preparation is key, and cutting corners can lead to less-wearable garments. It really is worth the time and effort to slow down and prepare correctly. Let's do this!

HOW TO USE THIS BOOK

I really want this book to be accessible to all abilities, so I've written it with my younger self in mind. Think of me as your sewing 'big sister'. My eight dreamy dress projects can be found in order of difficulty, so you can work through at a level you feel comfortable with. You'll find technique tutorials peppered throughout the pages, with extra visuals to guide you through trickier techniques. If it's the styling you need help with, keep an eye out for my styling suggestions on how to put together dressier or more casual outfits with your garments, depending on your own personal style. And if that's not enough, you can head to my website, www.thecraftypie.com for a whole host of extra content to help you build your dream handmade wardrobe.

So, without further ado, let's get sewing!

PATTERNS

The patterns in this book are all in a PDF format and can be accessed using this QR code.

To print your patterns at home, select the A4 print-at-home option. Make sure your pages are set to 100% scale and are being printed single sided. You can print just the first page and measure the test box to ensure the pattern is being printed to the correct scale before printing the rest.

Once printed, you must stick the pages together according to the guide, making sure that all the markings align. You can use glue or tape to do this, depending on your preference.

For those short on time, you may prefer to send your patterns to be printed in A0 format by a professional printer. This means they will be returned to you in large sheets that are ready to be cut out straight away. As a busy mum, this is usually my preferred option!

Pattern size guides

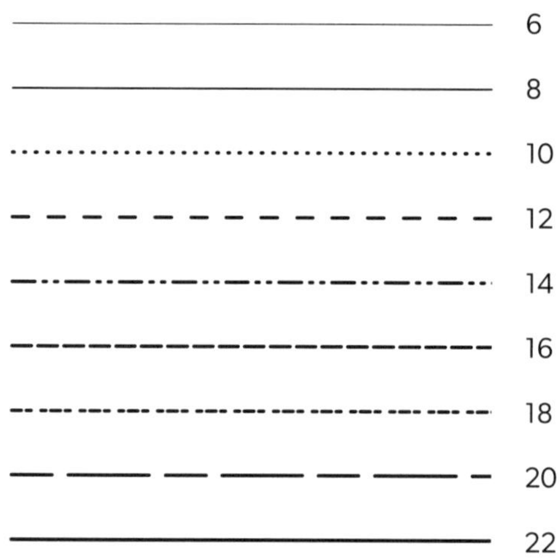

Once you've printed your pattern – and joined the pages together if you've printed it at home – measure yourself to assess which size fits you best (see page 24) and then cut out the pattern pieces carefully, following the cutting lines for your size as shown in the chart above.

MEASURING UP

This is arguably one of the most important steps as, obviously, we want our clothes to fit like they were made just for us! Grab your tape measure, carefully take your bust, waist and hip measurements and compare them to the size chart below. This is a great starting point, but please remember that all bodies are different. Once you have identified your size, refer to the finished measurements for each dress to check the overall fit and make any adjustments necessary.

Over the years, I have also learned how invaluable it is not only to look at the overall size chart, but the finished garment measurements too. All garments have different levels of ease: some may be more figure hugging, while others are intended to have a more relaxed fit. Once you've decided on your project, think about how you want the garment to fit you, depending on your preferences. The bigger the difference between the size chart and the finished garment measurements, the more loose-fitting your finished dress is designed to be. If you are between sizes, this may help you decide whether to size up or down.

If you have any doubts about the sizing or the fit, or if you are a beginner, I highly recommend that before you cut into an expensive fabric you consider making up a toile.

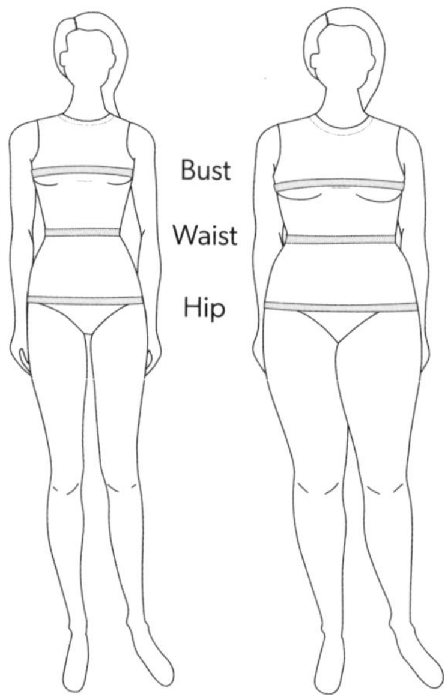

Standard ready-to-wear measurements

	6	8	10	12	14	16	18	20	22
Bust (cm)	78½	83	88	93	98	103	108	113	118
Bust (in)	31	32½	34½	36½	38½	40½	42½	44½	46½
Waist (cm)	60	64	69	74	79	84	89	94	99
Waist (in)	23½	25	27	29	31	33	35	37	39
Hip (cm)	86	90	95	100	105	110	115	120	125
Hip (in)	33¾	35½	37½	39½	41½	43¼	45¼	47¼	49¼

MAKING A TOILE

A toile is a fancy word for what is essentially a 'practice dress'. When I first started on my sewing journey, 99% of the time I would sew a toile first. It lets you test out the fit and practise the process without having to be worried about ruining any precious fabric. Just bear in mind that, where possible, your toile fabric should be the same blend and weight as your final fabric to give you the most accurate idea of the fit. As you develop your sewing skills, a toile becomes less necessary, especially on garments with lots of ease. But if you're hoping for that perfectly fitting dress, it really will be worth your time.

CHOOSING FABRIC

As well as preparing your pattern, you also need to gather your chosen fabric and notions for each project. I make some suggestions with each pattern, but make sure to consult my Fabric Focus guide (see page 14) as well to help you choose something suitable.

PRE-WASHING FABRIC

I get asked a lot on my socials about pre-washing fabric and whether it's a necessary step, and my answer will always be yes. This is coming from someone who has spent hours on a dress, only to shrink it to half the size in the first wash…

Pre-washing fabric ensures that any shrinkage happens prior to cutting out and sewing up your garment, and also eliminates any dyes or fibres that may transfer to other clothing before washing. I generally opt for a 30-degree gentle wash and air-dry on an airer, as this is how my handmade clothes will generally be washed between wears too, but it's always wise to check the washing instructions of each particular fabric as well. You can ask your fabric seller directly for advice on this or check in the product-description box if shopping online.

CUTTING OUT

Once both your fabric and pattern pieces are prepared, we can move on to cutting out. The tools needed for this are completely down to personal choice. Some sewers like to use pins and sharp dressmaking scissors for this, whereas others prefer to use a rotary cutter on a self-healing cutting mat. Both are great options, so just choose whatever you feel most comfortable with.

To begin, iron your fabric to get rid of any creases, then lay it out on a flat surface. Fold it in half with right sides together, lining up the selvedge (this is the finished edge of the fabric that keeps it from fraying, which often has a border running down it). Smooth the fabric out so there are no folds or puckers, and if it has a directional pattern, such as stripes, ensure that both layers of fabric are properly aligned.

Use the layout guide to place the pattern pieces right-side up on the fabric and hold in place with pins or pattern weights. Take care to read the pattern markings and follow the cutting layouts carefully as some pieces may need to be placed on the fold or cut from a single layer of fabric. Use your preferred cutting tool to cut around the pattern pieces and use smaller scissors to cut into any notches. Transfer any markings such as darts to the fabric using chalk or a removable fabric pen.

Note that the cutting layouts are designed to make the most out of your fabric and assume that you are using a non-directional print. If your fabric pattern has an obvious top and bottom, you may need extra fabric and should cut your pattern pieces with that in mind.

It's almost time for some sewing, yay!

MACHINE PREP

The final step is to prepare your machine. Choose your desired thread colour, wind up your bobbin and thread your machine. Think about the weight and thickness of your fabric, as you may need to change the weight of your machine needle or your presser-foot pressure to reflect this.

Are you sewing with stretch fabric? You'll want a ballpoint needle, and consider whether you need to swap out your regular presser foot for a walking foot. Head to my technique tutorial, Sewing with Stretch (see page 46) for some extra tips!

Top tip!

If you've made it through all those steps, hooray! It may seem like a lot of work, but you'll thank me later. You're one step closer to having your dream handmade wardrobe. Now let's head to the machine...

THE PROJECTS

You've done all your prep, now it's time for the sewing! The garments are laid out in a rough order of difficulty so feel free to choose your first project based on your own level of ability. Pay close attention to the technique tutorials which will guide you through the trickiest parts. And, above all, enjoy it sewers!

THE T-SHIRT DRESS

Everyday style, asymmetric waistline

I love the versatility of a T-shirt dress, and it's the perfect entry-level sewing project. Get creative with an asymmetrical waistline and a contrast skirt, or keep it simple and opt for the mini with a classic bodice seam. A cotton skirt will add a dressier look, or go casual with all jersey. You can sew this up on an overlocker or regular machine depending on your preference and what you have to work with.

Fabric suggestions

- Light-/medium-weight jersey or knit with at least 10% two-way stretch
- Light-/medium-weight cotton for the contrasting skirt variation

Notions

- 1m (1yd) of fabric for the bodice, 150cm (60in) wide
- 1.25m (1½yd) of fabric for the skirt, 150cm (60in) wide
- Ballpoint/stretch sewing-machine needle
- Optional: fusible seam tape

Top tip!

When using fabrics with directional prints – especially large, obvious patterns – you may need extra fabric so you can arrange your pattern pieces on the fabric to get the best out of your print.

Notes

- All seams should be sewn with a 1cm (⅜in) seam allowance unless otherwise stated. On a regular sewing machine, when working with stretch fabrics, as here, this should be done with a zigzag stitch roughly 2.5mm long and 1.5mm wide. If using an overlocker, you will need to trim off the excess seam allowances by following the guide on your machine while sewing.
- Check out my technique tutorials on sewing with stretch (page 46) and gathering (page 64) before you begin.
- Conversions to imperial measurements aren't always precise as they often need to be rounded up or down, but they do work with the patterns. Stick with either the metric or imperial measurements – don't mix and match.

Finished measurements

	6	8	10	12	14	16	18	20	22
Bust (cm)	90	95	100	105	110	115	120	125	130
Bust (in)	35½	37½	39½	41½	43½	45¼	47¼	49¼	51
Waist (cm)	90	95	100	105	110	115	120	125	130
Waist (in)	35½	37½	39½	41½	43½	45¼	47¼	49¼	51
Front hem width (cm)	101	103.5	106	108.5	111	113.5	116	118.5	121
Front hem width (in)	39¾	40¾	41¾	42¾	43¾	44½	45½	46½	47½
Front length (cm)	88.5	89.1	89.7	90.3	90.9	91.5	92.1	92.7	93.3
Front length (in)	34¾	35	35¼	35½	35¾	36	36¼	36½	36¾
Sleeve length (cm)	21.5	22	22.5	23	23.5	24	24.5	25	25.5
Sleeve length (in)	8½	8⅝	8¾	9	9¼	9½	9⅝	9¾	10

Cutting guide

1 Asymmetric bodice front – cut 1

2 Asymmetric bodice back – cut 1

3 Asymmetric skirt front – cut 1

4 Asymmetric skirt back – cut 1

5 Sleeve – cut 2

6 Neckline binding – cut 1

All sizes: 150cm (60in) wide skirt fabric

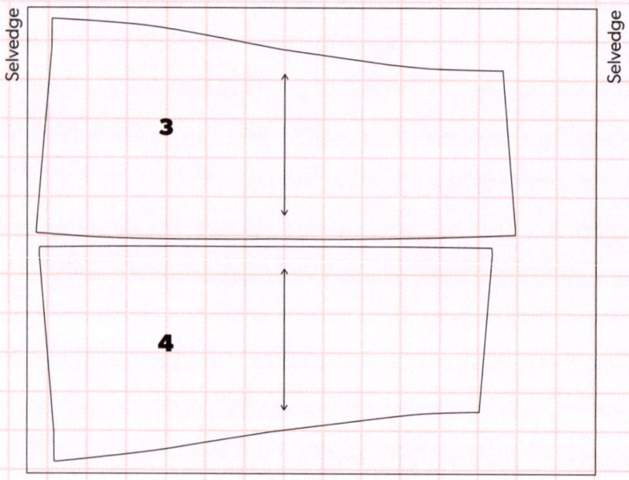

All sizes: 150cm (60in) wide bodice fabric

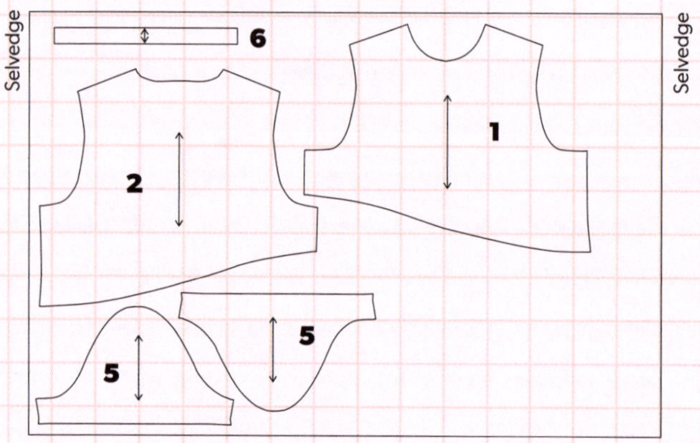

Stitching the shoulders & neck

1 Cut out the fabric pieces and transfer markings. Place the bodice front on top of the bodice back with right sides together and pin the shoulder seams in place. Stitch together on your sewing machine or overlocker. If using a sewing machine, trim the seam allowance in half once sewn. If using an overlocker, the seam allowance will automatically be trimmed for you. Press the seam allowance towards the back bodice. (FYI: jersey doesn't press as well as woven fabrics, but I still like to press all seams after sewing them to keep everything looking neat.)

2 Fold the neckband in half, bringing the short ends right sides together, and stitch the seam. Trim the seam allowance if necessary. Press the seam open.

3 Now fold the neckband in half, lengthways this time, bringing the wrong sides together. Give it a quick press to keep this fold in place.

4 The seam in the neckband goes at the centre back. Find the centre front of the neckband by folding it in half with the seam at one end and then place a pin in the fold at the other end – this pin marks the centre front.

5 Match the centre-back seam of the neckband to the notch on the bodice-back neckline and pin in place. Then match the centre front of the neckband to the notch on the bodice-front neckline.

6 Continue to pin the rest of the band to the neckline as evenly as possible. As the band is slightly shorter, you'll need to stretch it to fit. Use lots of pins.

7 Stitch the neckband in place, stretching it as you sew, while trying to avoid any stretching of the neckline underneath. If using an overlocker for this, stitch it on without cutting off any seam allowance; if using a regular machine, sew it with a 0.5cm (¼in) seam allowance.

1

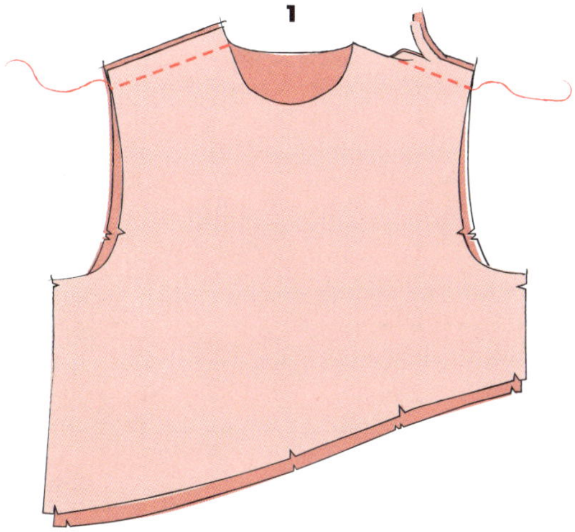

2

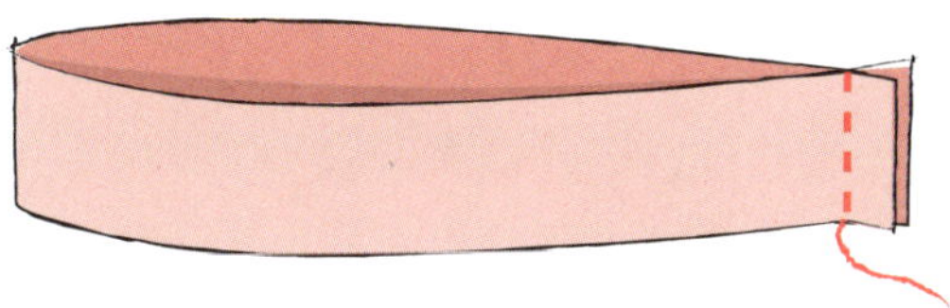

3

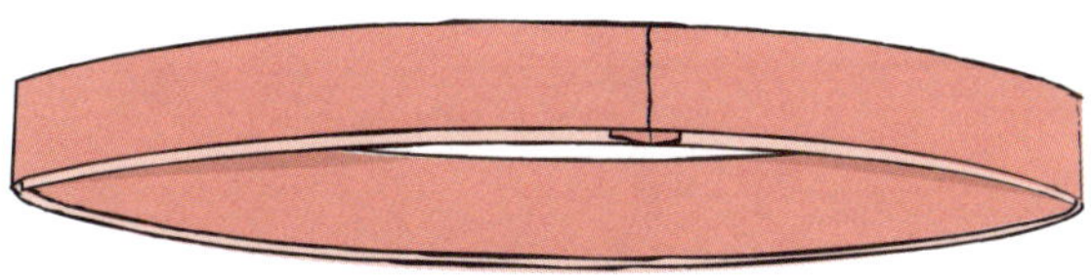

6

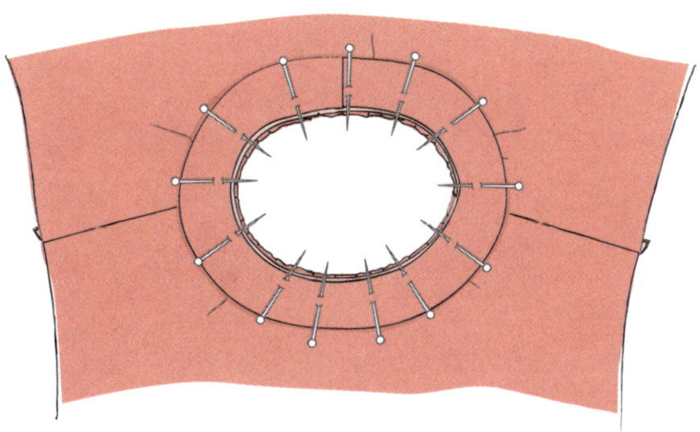

8 Check you have no puckers in your neckline. Once happy with the result, press the seam allowance down and away from the neckline. The steam will also help to bring in any unwanted stretching.

Inserting the sleeves

9 Lay your bodice flat on a table with the right side facing up. Lay the sleeves right-side up on the correct side of the bodice, making sure that the single and double notches match.

10 Flip one sleeve over so it's laying right sides together with the bodice. Pin together at the notches and both ends before evenly distributing the rest of the sleeve head in the armhole. Stitch the sleeve in place. I prefer to do this on my regular machine before moving to my overlocker. Repeat with the second sleeve then finish or trim the seam allowance as desired.

Finishing the bodice

11 Place the bodice front and back together with right sides facing and pin at one side seam, then continue up along the underarm seam of the sleeve. Repeat on the other side seam and sleeve. Stitch the seams on your sewing machine or overlocker with one continuous seam, all the way from the bottom of the bodice to the sleeve edge. Trim the seam allowances, if necessary, and press to the back.

12 Try on your bodice to check you're happy with the overall fit. If it's a little loose, feel free to stitch the side seams again with a wider seam allowance. You also need to check the length of the sleeve. Remember, it will be 1.5cm (⅝in) shorter once the hem is sewn.

10

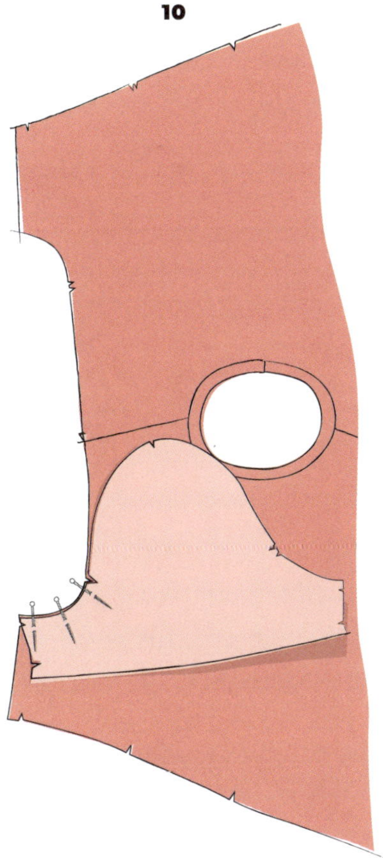

11

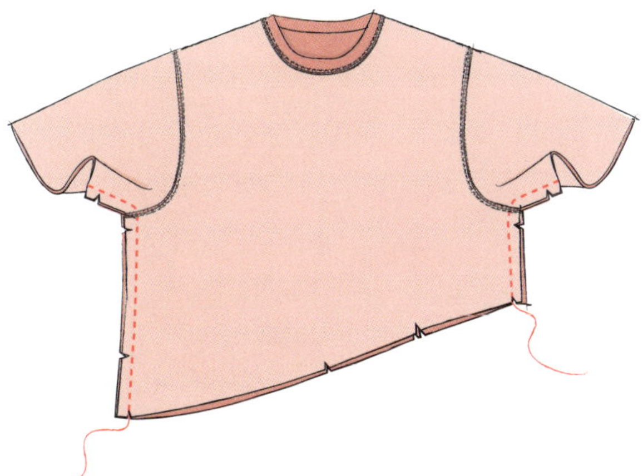

Hemming the sleeves

13 Finish the raw edge of the sleeve hem with your overlocker, if you're using one. Press the hem under by 1.5cm (⅝in) and pin in place. Stitch this down 1.2cm (½in) away from the edge of the sleeve with zigzag stitch (or see the tip below).

Top tip!

Want to create an ultra-professional finish? Sew your sleeve and skirt hems with a twin needle and straight stitch instead of a zigzag stitch for that high-end look. The bobbin thread zigzags between the two needle threads, so you still get the stretch that you need in your stitch.

Attaching the skirt

14 Lay the skirt front and back right sides together and pin along each side seam, matching the notches. Stitch on your sewing machine or overlocker, then trim the seam allowance, if necessary. Press the seam allowance towards the back.

15 Now we need to gather the skirt to be the same width as the bodice. Run two rows of gathering stitches along the waistline edge of both the skirt front and back (see my technique tutorial on gathering on page 64). Make sure to leave a long tail of thread on each end.

16 Turn your bodice inside out to allow you to place the bottom edge right sides together with the top of the skirt. Carefully match the side seams and pin in place. You also need to match the centre front and back notches and pin.

15

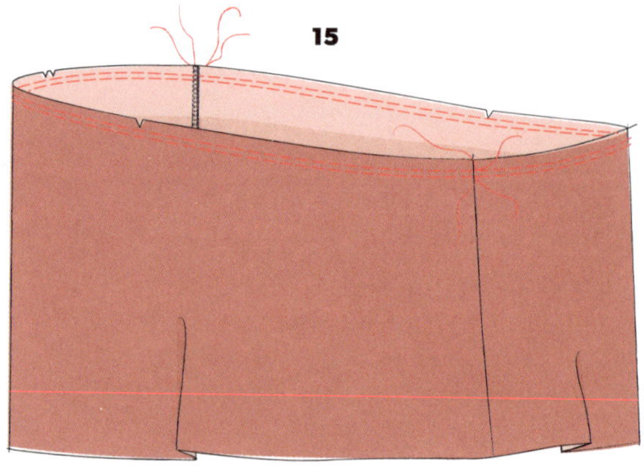

17

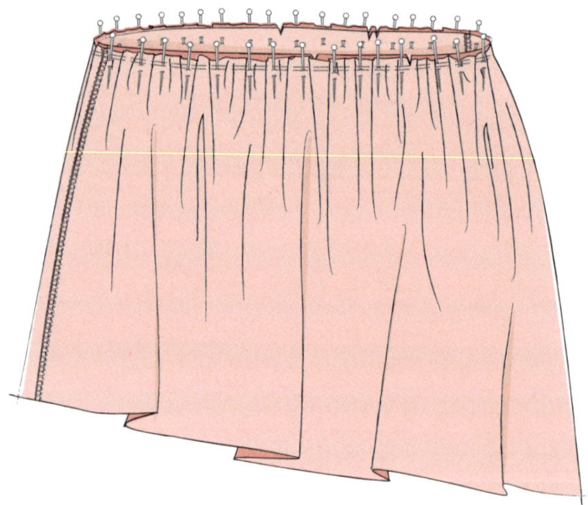

17 Now you can see how much of the skirt fabric you need to gather. Carefully pull on the thread tails that we left in step 15 to gather in the fabric and evenly distribute it between the pins. You will need to use lots of pins to keep this securely in place. Do this all the way round the skirt before stitching the seam. Finish the raw edges on your overlocker or with zigzag stitch on your regular sewing machine.

18 Check that you're happy with the seam and that the gathers are all laying nice and flat, then unpick the row of gathering stitches that falls outside of the seam allowance.

Top tip!

When sewing a gathered edge, particularly if using a woven fabric paired with the jersey bodice, you may find the fabric stretches along the waistline. As an extra precaution, you can use seam tape. Baste or fuse this to the seam allowance of the bodice before gathering and attaching the skirt, and it will add some extra stability, and hopefully reduce any wavy seams.

Finishing touches

19 Give everything a good press, including the waist seam, which should be pressed upwards towards the bodice.

20 Have a final try on. Feel free to cut the skirt down to the desired length, remembering that the hem will be 1.5cm (⅝in) shorter once sewn.

21 For both the woven and stretch skirt fabrics, finish the raw edge of the hem with an overlocker if you have one, then press the hem under by 1.5cm (⅝in) and pin in place. Stitch at 1.2cm (½in) away from the hem edge with zigzag stitch or using a twin needle.

Woo!

You did it! You tackled the very first project! Now go swish around in your brand-new dress!

Styling suggestion

Wanting to elevate your look for a girl's night out? Pair your T-shirt Dress with matching heels and a bag that will bring a pop of contrasting colour. Even better if you have a matching lipstick too!

VARIATION

Classic waistline

Sometimes you just want a classic dress that you can throw on and feel comfortable in, while still looking cute. This is it for me! Make the dress in all-jersey or play around with a plain bodice and patterned skirt for some extra interest. The choice is up to you!

Cutting guide

1 Straight-waist bodice front – cut 1 on fold
2 Straight-waist bodice back – cut 1 on fold
3 Straight-waist skirt front – cut 1 on fold
4 Straight-waist skirt back – cut 1 on fold
5 Sleeve – cut 2
6 Neckline binding – cut 1

All sizes: 150cm (60in) wide fabric

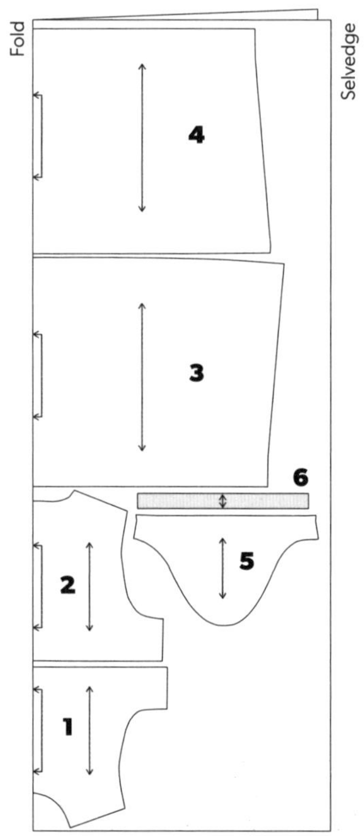

Notions

- 1m (1yd) of fabric for the bodice, 150cm (60in) wide
- 1.25m (1½yd) of fabric for the skirt, 150cm (60in) wide
- Ballpoint/stretch sewing-machine needle
- Optional: fusible seam tape

Making the variation

1 Cut our your pattern pieces, making sure to choose the bodice front and back with the straight waistline and the same for the skirt pieces.

2 Construct the dress in exactly the same way as the asymmetrical version, following the instructions on pages 35–41.

Top tip!

This dress will be easiest to make with the straight waistline and fully in jersey, so maybe start with that if you're new to this. Sewing a mixture of stretch and woven fabrics can pose some challenges when it comes to avoiding any stretching at the waistline, so be extra careful if you do opt for contrasting fabrics.

Technique Tutorial: *Sewing with stretch*

As a beginner, sewing with stretch can seem daunting, but it doesn't have to be! Here are my top tips for tackling those stretch fabrics.

Change your needle

Most craft shops stock specialist jersey needles that help glide through jersey fabrics and prevent unnecessary stretching. They are universal and can easily be inserted by unscrewing your old needle and replacing it. All machines are slightly different so make sure to consult your machine manual for specific instructions on how to do this.

Set the presser-foot pressure

The presser foot is what controls your fabric as it feeds through the machine, so if this is using too much pressure, it can cause your fabric to stretch out as you sew. There are a few ways to tackle this:

- Reduce your presser-foot pressure. How you do this depends on the make and model of your machine, so refer to your manual.
- Try out a walking-foot attachment. This helps the fabric feed through more evenly and reduces the stretch. Some machine models, like my Pfaff Passport, even offer this option built in.
- Pick a stretch setting on your machine. This isn't available on all models, but higher end machines sometimes offer the option to select a setting that is specifically for stretch that will automatically adjust things like the stitch length and presser-foot pressure for you.

Use a zigzag stitch

Our jersey garments need to be able to stretch as we wear them. A regular straight stitch won't allow this stretch to happen and therefore the stitches will burst as we move around. Make sure to select a zigzag stitch which will allow the fabric to move with your body. If you're unfamiliar with using this stitch, it's always a good idea to sew a few practice seams on some scrap fabric. And don't just opt for the default zigzag stitch – you're not doing appliqué – I recommend a stitch roughly 2.5mm long and 1.5mm wide.

Upgrade to an overlocker/serger

If you've been sewing for a while and plan to use a lot of stretch fabrics, it may be worth investing in an overlocker. These machines tend to handle stretch a lot better and most seams can be sewn directly on there, without the need for your regular machine. It can make stretch projects super speedy and your garments more durable.

Don't forget the steam

Stretch projects can often look worse before they look better, so don't be disheartened if you see a few wavy seams. Grab your iron and give the seam a press with lots of steam. This will shrink the fabric back in and, more often than not, it will completely eliminate any stretching that has occurred!

Have confidence

Sometimes with sewing you just have to throw yourself in and believe in yourself. We all have to start somewhere, and practice really does make perfect. If it's your first-ever time sewing with stretch, don't expect perfection. Try a toile, make some mistakes, and remind yourself that it's all a learning process if things don't quite go to plan. You'll get there in the end, I promise!

Take a break

If all else fails and you're starting to get frustrated, make yourself a cuppa and come back to the project another day. It's amazing what a break from a project and a fresh pair of eyes can do.

Overlocker/serger

Zigzag stitch

THE SUN DRESS

Tiered maxi, long straps, shirred back

This dress is the perfect, relaxed style to throw on for those warm summer days, or to layer up with a cute denim jacket and trainers. The design is based on a self-drafted dress that I wore non-stop last year and I'm so excited for it to be included in the book. In order for it to be ultra versatile, this pattern offers mini and midi versions as well as the maxi-length dress, but I encourage you to play around with the dimensions of the rectangles for the skirt tiers to find your perfect silhouette.

Fabric suggestions

- Viscose
- Cotton/polycotton (I am obsessed with a large-scale gingham for this dress!)
- Linen/linen blends
- Double gauze fabric

Notions

- 5.5m (6yd) of main fabric, 150cm (60in) wide, for the maxi version or 3.5m (4yd) of main fabric, 150cm (60in) wide, for the midi version without the bottom skirt tier
- 0.5m (½yd) of lining fabric, 150cm (60in) wide
- A few reels of shirring elastic in a colour to complement your dress

Notes

- All seams should be sewn with a 1cm (⅜in) seam allowance unless otherwise stated.
- Check out my technique tutorials on gathering (page 64), shirring (page 122) and understitching (page 178) before you begin.
- Conversions to imperial measurements aren't always precise as they often need to be rounded up or down, but they do work with the patterns. Stick with either the metric or imperial measurements – don't mix and match.

Finished measurements

	6	8	10	12	14	16	18	20	22
Bust (cm)	86.6	91.6	96.6	101.6	106.6	111.6	116.6	121.6	126.6
Bust (in)	34	36	38	40	42	44	46	48	50
Waist (cm)	74	79	84	89	94	99	104	109	114
Waist (in)	29	31	33	35	37	39	41	43	45
Front hem width (cm)	292	294.5	297	299.5	302	304.5	307	309.5	312
Front hem width (in)	115	116	117	118	119	120	121	122	123
Front length (cm)	119.3	119.3	119.3	119.3	119.3	119.3	119.3	119.3	119.3
Front length (in)	47	47	47	47	47	47	47	47	47
Strap length (cm)	120	120.6	121.2	121.8	122.4	123	123.6	124.2	124.8
Strap length (in)	47¼	47½	47¾	48	48¼	48½	48¾	49	49¼

Cutting guide

1 Bodice front – cut 1 main and 1 lining on fold

2 Bodice back panel – to be shirred – cut 1

3 Bodice side back – cut 2 main and 2 lining

4 Straps – cut 4

5 Bodice back template – cut 1 after shirring the fabric

6 Upper tier: skirt front – cut 1 on fold

7 Upper tier: skirt back – cut 1 on fold

8 Middle tier: skirt front – cut 1 on fold

9 Middle tier: skirt side – cut 2

10 Middle tier: back skirt – cut 2

11 Lower tier, maxi version: centre front – cut 1 on fold

12 Lower tier, maxi version: skirt side front and back – cut 10

All sizes: 150cm (60in) wide main fabric

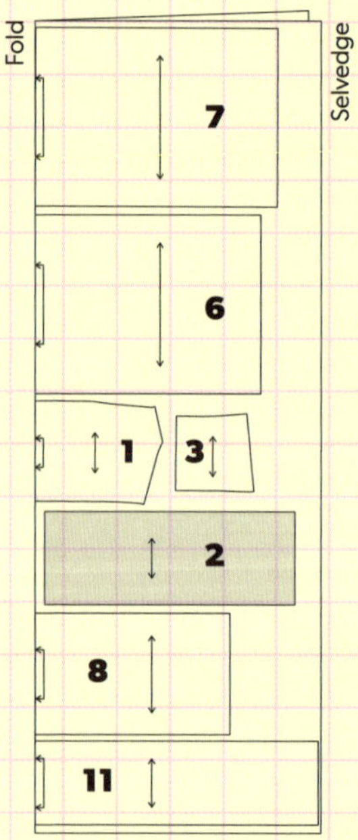

Lining fabric

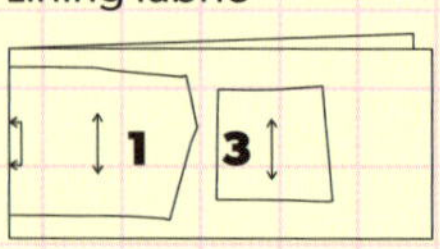

Shirred fabric

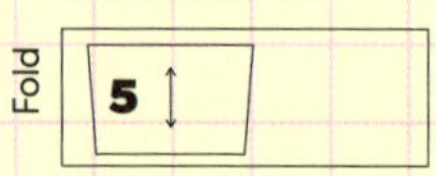

All sizes: 150cm (60in) wide main fabric

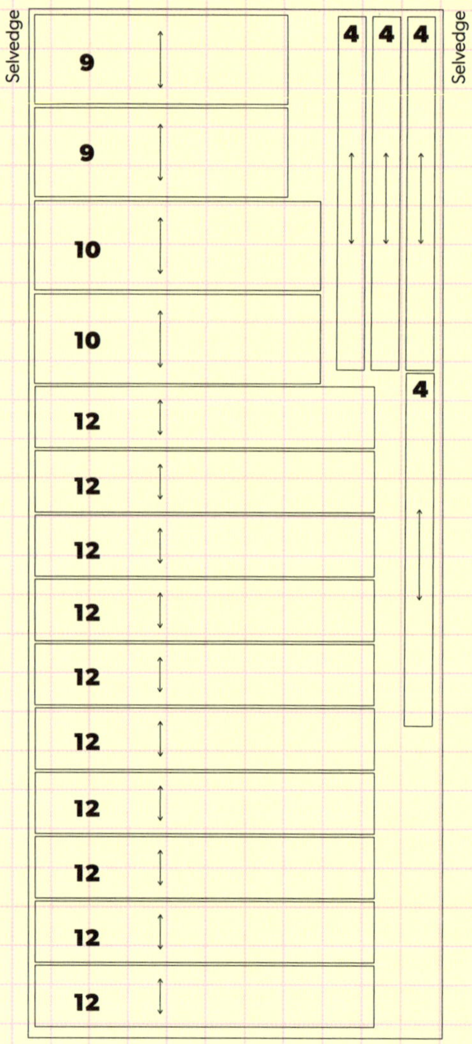

Top tip!

To allow for some epic swishing, the skirt tiers are made up of panels. Use the diagrams below to help you visualize how they go together. (For the midi version, omit the lower tier.)

Middle Tier

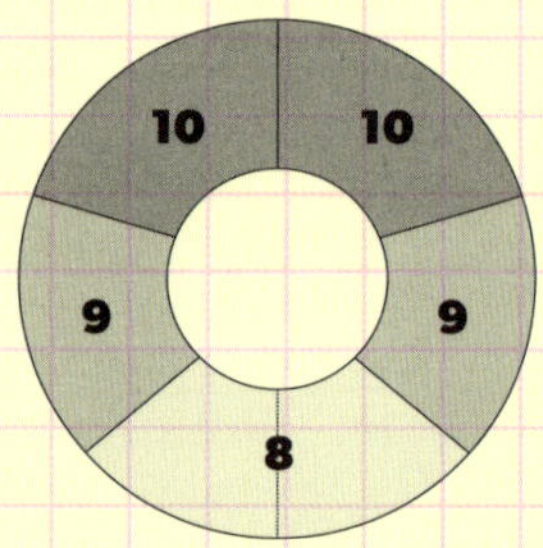

Lower Tier

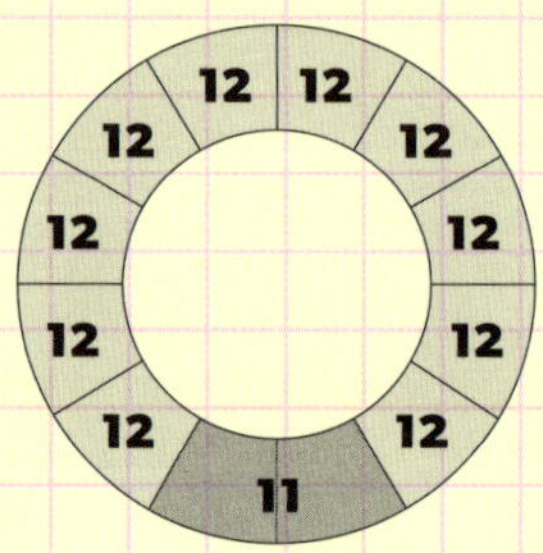

Preparing the front bodice

1 Cut out the fabric pieces and transfer markings. Sew the darts on the bodice front, leaving a long tail of thread to tie off the end, and press the darts down towards the waistline.

2 Next, sew the front bodice to the bodice side back pieces. Finish the raw edges and press towards the back. Repeat for the lining.

Preparing the straps

3 Fold each of the straps in half lengthways with right sides together.

4 Sew along the length of the strap, pivot and continue along the short end. Leave the other short end open to turn the strap out.

4

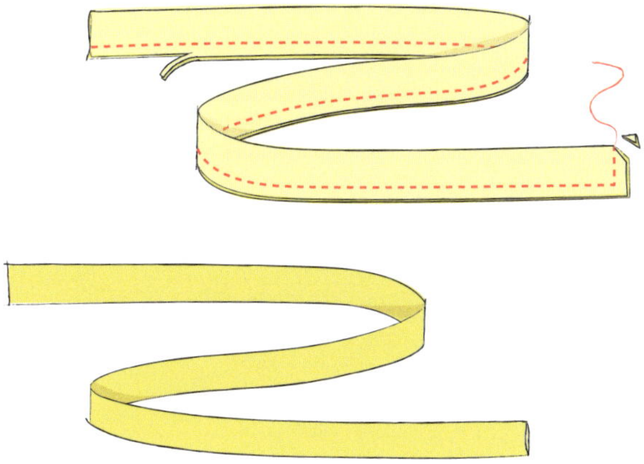

5 Clip the corners of the seam allowances, trim the seam allowances down to 0.5cm (¼in) and turn the strap out. You may need to use something pointy, like a knitting needle, to push out the corners fully. Press well.

6 Align each strap with the notches on the bodice front and side back. Pin in place on the right side of the bodice and baste.

6

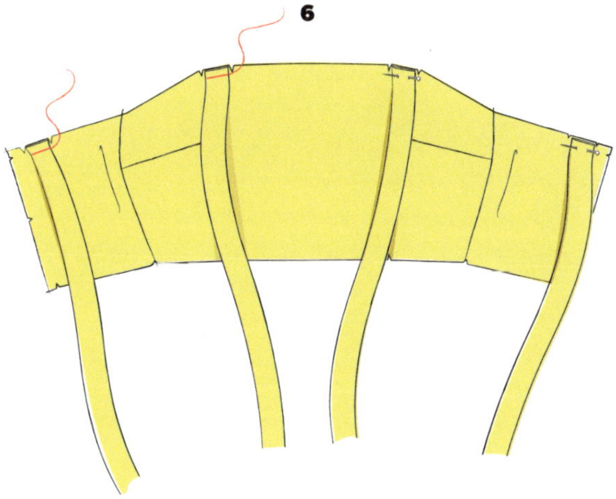

Preparing the shirred back panel

7 Finish the top edge of the back bodice panel by overlocking the raw edge and pressing it under by 0.5cm (¼in) before topstitching.

7

8 Swap out the regular thread on your bobbin for shirring elastic. Up your stitch length to its maximum and, using a scrap piece of fabric, play around with your tension until the fabric is gathering evenly.

9 Begin shirring the panel, sewing each row 1cm (⅜in) apart and following the pattern markings (see page 122 for further help). If you struggle to sew in a straight line, you may want to draw lines directly onto the fabric with a removable pen (like a Pilot Frixion pen) to help you stay in line.

10 Once completely shirred, place the back-bodice template on top of the shirred panel, pin in place, aligning the hemmed edge with the top of the pattern piece, and cut out. It may be easier to do this with a rotary cutter to prevent any shifting of the fabric.

10

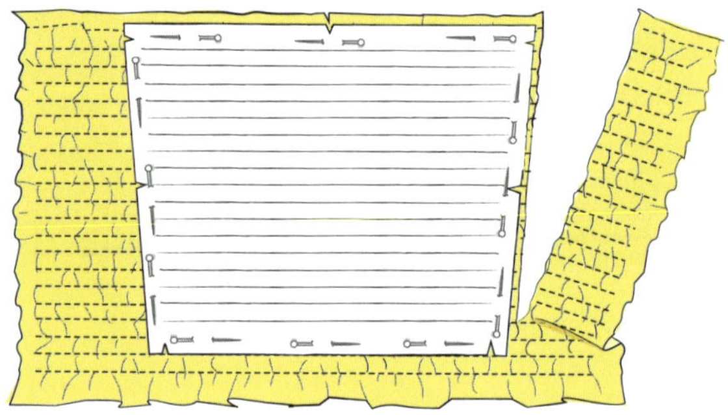

Constructing the bodice

11 With right sides together, pin the bodice lining to the main bodice and stitch along the top edge with your regular 1cm (⅜in) seam allowance. Understitch the seam allowance to the lining (see page 178) and press to the back.

11

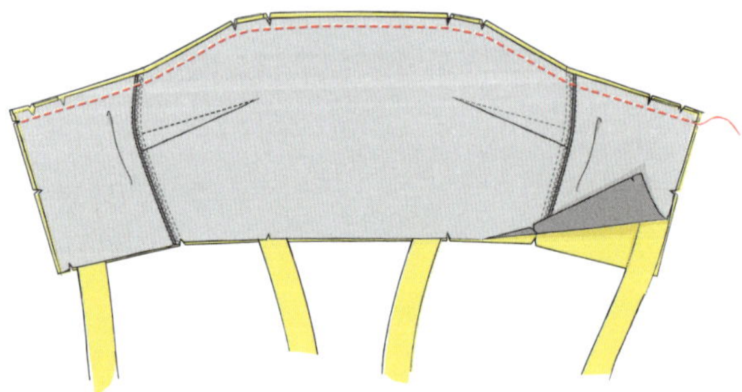

12 With right sides together, pin the bodice side back pieces to the shirred back panel and stitch in place, making sure the top edges of the back and side-back bodice line up exactly. Finish the raw edges and press towards the back.

Attaching the skirt

13 With right sides facing, stitch the upper tier skirt front and back together at the side seams. Finish the seam allowance and press towards the back.

14 Run two rows of gathering stitches along the waistline of the skirt (see my technique tutorial on gathering on page 64).

15 Starting at one of the side seams, gather the front skirt to be the same width as the front bodice and pin in place with right sides facing.

16 For the back skirt, no gathering is needed across the shirred panel, as this will create gathers on its own. Start by pinning the centre back of the skirt to the centre back of the shirred panel. Stretch out the shirring and pin the skirt along the waistline edge. Once you reach the end of the shirring, begin your gathering, and continue to pin round to the side seam on each side.

14

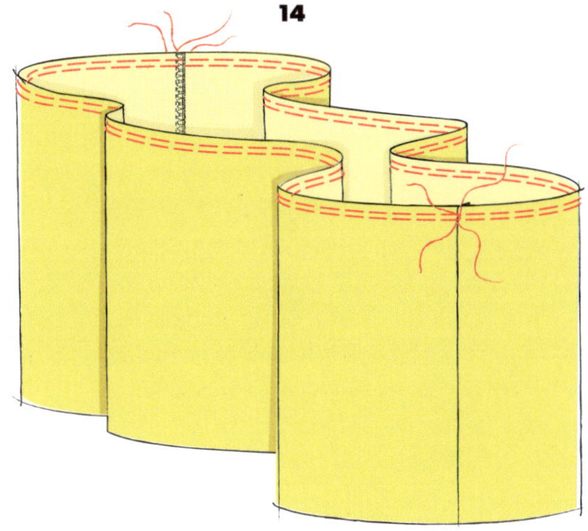

16

17 Stitch the skirt in place, being careful to keep the gathers even. Finish the seam allowances and press them upwards.

18 Repeat this process for the other skirt tiers, first joining the panels for each tier together along their side edges, referring to the diagrams on page 52. Run gathering stitches along the top edge of each tier, as in step 14 and then match the centre points of the front tiers before evenly spreading out the gathers all the way round. Stitch in place.

Top tip!

If you're unsure on the dimensions of your tiers, try on your dress after adding each one. Each skirt piece is a simple rectangle, so it is fine to cut the length down as necessary to produce your dream dress!

Finishing touches

19 Have a final try on of your dress to make sure you are happy with the overall fit and length. Make your final adjustments as necessary.

20 To hem the dress, press under 0.5cm (¼in) and then 1cm (⅜in). Stitch down at 0.8cm (5⁄16in) away from the hem edge to create the perfect double hem.

Woo!

You did it! You're now the proud owner of the perfect sun dress for all occasions. I absolutely love to see your finished makes. Why not upload a selfie to Instagram and tag me @the_crafty_pie for the sewing community to see?

Styling suggestion

Lacking some sun? Don't be afraid to layer up your dress for colder days. I love to pair my sun dress with a plain white tee underneath for a more casual look that's suitable for spring.

VARIATION

Mini-length, short straps

Flaunt that golden summer glow with this mini variation of the sun dress. You've only got one skirt piece to attach, so it's a quicker sew that's also wonderfully cool and light to wear in those warmer months. The straps are shorter and more practical in this version, but feel free to mix and match the pattern pieces as desired to create your dream summer dress.

Finished measurements

	6	8	10	12	14	16	18	20	22
Front hem width (cm)	104	106.5	109	111.5	114	116.5	119	121.5	124
Front hem width (in)	41	42	43	44	45	46	47	48	49
Front length (cm)	69.3	69.3	69.3	69.3	69.3	69.3	69.3	69.3	69.3
Front length (in)	27¼	27¼	27¼	27¼	27¼	27¼	27¼	27¼	27¼
Strap length (cm)	60	60.6	61.2	61.8	62.4	63	63.6	64.2	64.8
Strap length (in)	23½	23¾	24	24¼	24½	24¾	25	25¼	25½

Notions

- 2m (2¼yd) of main fabric, 150cm (60in) wide
- 0.5m (½yd) of lining fabric, 150cm (60in) wide
- A few reels of shirring elastic in a colour to complement your dress

Making the variation

1 Cut out your pattern pieces, making sure to choose the correct strap length according to your preference. You only have the upper skirt tier to cut out when following the mini variation.

2 Begin to construct the dress in exactly the same way as the maxi.

3 When you reach the section about attaching the skirt, simply sew on the top tier and ignore any references to additional tiers.

4 Try on your dress to check the fit before hemming the bottom of your mini as normal with a double-turned hem (see step 20 of the maxi dress instructions to turn the hem).

Top tip!

Even if you don't normally feel comfortable wearing mini-length garments day-to-day, don't overlook this variation! It can easily be styled with some trousers for a comfortable, everyday look.

Technique Tutorial: *Gathering*

To say I'm a fan of gathering would be an understatement! This technique is used to reduce the width of fabric and is most commonly seen in voluminous skirts and puff sleeves. Most of the projects in this book involve some kind of gathering, so let's get into how to produce perfect gathers. We'll use a skirt that we will gather and attach to a bodice as an example.

1 To begin, we must sew gathering stitches across the width of fabric that we wish to gather in. We want long stitches for this, so increase the stitch length of your machine to its maximum.

2 Now sew two rows of gathering stitches across the top of the skirt piece, one just within the seam allowance and once just outside of the seam allowance. As we are generally using a 1cm (⅜in) seam allowance throughout this book, this means your rows of stitching should be at 0.8cm (¼in) and 1.2cm (½in) from the edge of your fabric. We sew two rows of stitches rather than one as it helps to produce more even gathers and it makes it easier to sew over the gathers that form.

3 Make sure to leave a long tail of thread at each end as we will need this to pull up the gathers.

4 Now gather the skirt to become the same width as the bodice. Pin the skirt to the bodice with right sides together, matching the side seams, and then match the centre front and back points. This will clearly show you how much fabric you have to gather in.

5

7

8

5 Gently pull on the thread tails we left. You will see the fabric begin to gather. Use your fingers to push the gathers along the fabric and evenly spread them out. This is one of the most important steps, so take your time, and don't forget to use plenty of pins to hold the fabric in place.

6 Now sew the seam with a regular 1cm (⅜in) seam allowance, which will fall directly between your two rows of gathering stitches. Sew slowly, removing the pins as you go along. Try to ensure all the gathers are going directly downwards and not being dragged along as you sew. Don't be scared to stop and redistribute some of the gathers, as necessary.

7 Once sewn, turn the skirt the right way out and check you are happy with the way the gathers are looking. Unpick and resew any sections that may need it.

8 Finally, finish your raw edges and press the seam up. Unpick the visible row of gathering stitches that fell on the outside of the seam allowance.

And that's it! For beginner sewers, gathering is an essential technique to master and can really upgrade the final look of your garments when done well. Take your time, and remember to pin, pin, pin!

THE TEA DRESS

Bias-cut, midi-length, cap sleeves

I often look to luxury fashion brands for sewing inspiration, and the idea for this dress came straight from the catwalks. I have always loved how timeless a bias-cut dress can be, but wanted to add in a fun option to play around with colours and prints to create a truly unique piece. Sew it up all in one colour for the perfect wardrobe basic or go wild with prints for a stand-out dress.

Fabric suggestions

- Viscose/viscose sateen
- Silky satin
- Rayon

Notions

- Sizes 6–14: 0.7m (¾yd) of bodice fabric, 150cm (60in) wide. Sizes 16–22: 0.8m (1yd) of bodice fabric, 150cm (60in) wide
- Sizes 6–14: 1.4m (1½yd) of skirt fabric, 150cm (60in) wide. Sizes 16–22: 1.6m (1¾yd) of skirt fabric, 150cm (60in) wide
- Extra-sharp/ballpoint sewing-machine needle (it really makes a difference)
- Handmade or ready-made bias binding, 13mm (½in) wide (see page 100 to make your own)
- 56cm (22in) invisible zip
- Hook-and-eye fastening
- Small ready-made bow, if desired
- Optional: rolled-hem foot

Notes

- All seams should be sewn with a 1cm (⅜in) seam allowance unless otherwise stated.
- Check out my technique tutorials on cutting and sewing on the bias (page 82), gathering (page 64) and invisible zips (page 142) before you begin.
- Conversions to imperial measurements aren't always precise as they often need to be rounded up or down, but they do work with the patterns. Stick with either the metric or imperial measurements – don't mix and match.

Finished measurements

	6	8	10	12	14	16	18	20	22
Bust (cm)	84	89	94	99	104	109	114	119	124
Bust (in)	33	35	37	39	41	43	45	47	49
Waist (cm)	72.4	77.4	82.4	87.4	92.4	97.4	102.4	107.4	112.4
Waist (in)	28½	30½	32½	34½	36½	38½	40½	42¼	44¼
Top hip (cm) 10cm from waist	86	91	96	101	106	111	116	121	126
Top hip (in) 4in from waist	34	36	37¾	39¾	41¾	43¾	45½	47½	49½
Low hip (cm) 20cm from waist	97	102	107	112	117	122	127	132	137
Low hip (in) 8in from waist	38	40	42	44	46	48	50	52	54
Front hem width (cm)	68.8	71.3	73.8	76.3	78.8	81.3	83.8	86.3	88.8
Front hem width (in)	27	28	29	30	31	32	33	34	35
Front length (cm)	122.3	122.9	123.5	124.1	124.7	125.3	125.9	126.5	127.1
Front length (in)	48	48¼	48½	48¾	49	49¼	49½	49¾	50
Sleeve length (cm)	11.5	11.9	12.3	12.7	13.1	13.5	13.9	14.3	14.7
Sleeve length (in)	4½	4⅝	4¾	5	5⅛	5¼	5½	5⅝	5¾

Cutting guide

1 Bodice front – cut 1 on fold
2 Bodice back – cut 2
3 Skirt front – cut 1 on fold
4 Skirt back – cut 2
5 Sleeve – cut 2
6 Armhole binding – cut 2
7 Neckline binding – cut 1

Note

The front and back bodice and the sleeves (pieces 1, 2 and 5) are cut on the straight grain, while all the other pieces are cut on the bias, at a 45-degree angle (see page 82).

All sizes: 150cm (60in) wide bodice fabric

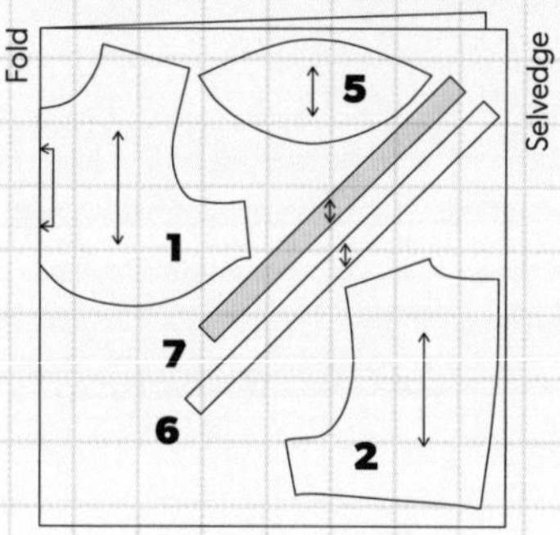

All sizes: 150cm (60in) wide skirt fabric

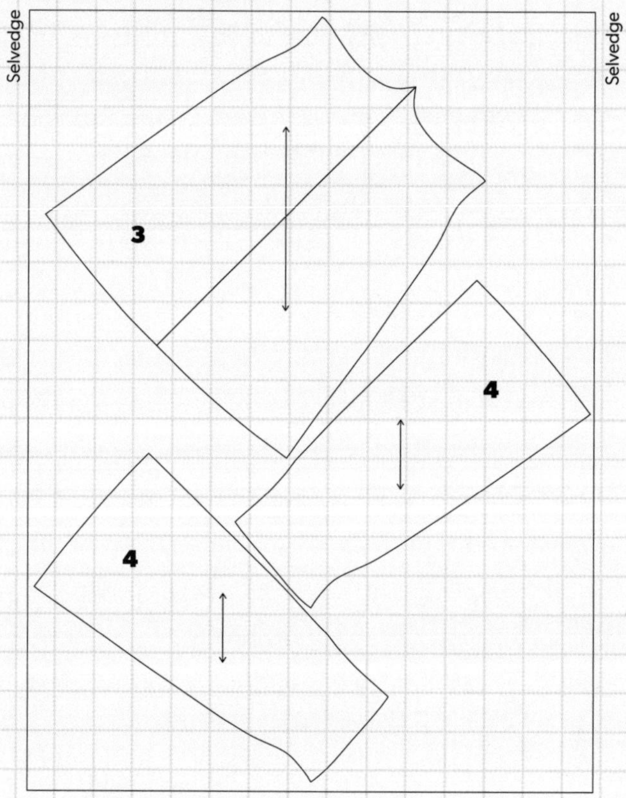

Pattern prep

1 Cut out the fabric pieces and transfer markings. Sew a line of stay stitching at 1cm (⅜in) along the neckline of the front and back bodice, and the side seams of the front and back skirt to prevent any stretching as you sew (see pages 19 and 83).

2

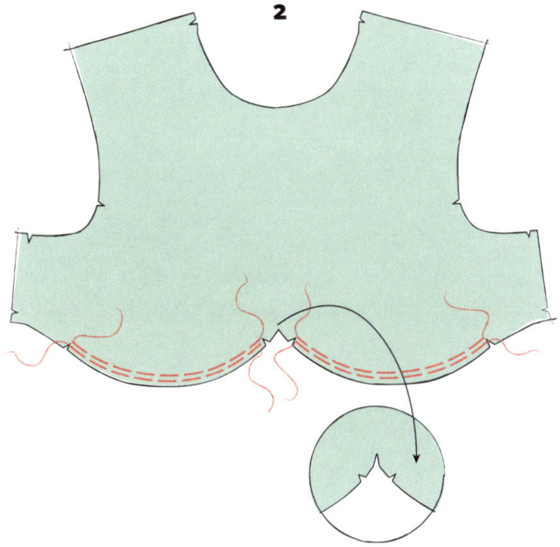

Attaching the bodice to the skirt

2 Run two rows of gathering stitches between the notches along the bust line on the bodice front, leaving a long thread tail at each end (see my technique tutorial on gathering on page 64).

3 Pin the bodice front to the skirt front along the bust line with right sides together. Start by matching the notches and then work round to pin the centre front.

4

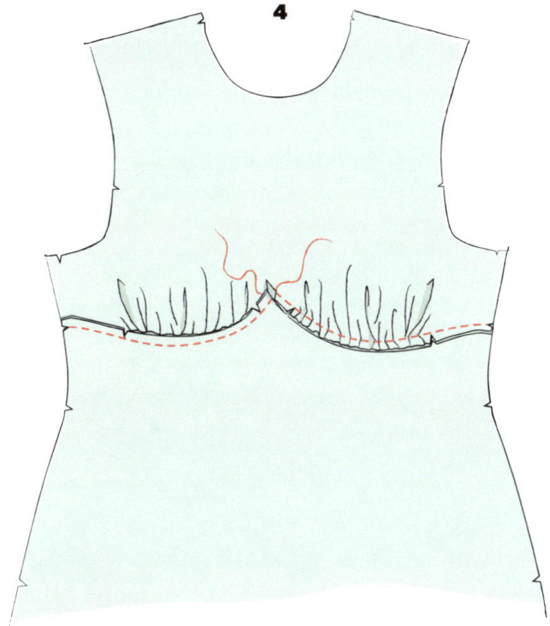

4 Sew the seam: start from the side seam and sew inwards towards the centre front – stop sewing at the centre point. Repeat this step, sewing from the opposite side inwards. It's easy to end up with puckers in your fabric at the centre point. If this happens, gently unpick your stitches and try again. A good steam afterwards will help reduce any stretching that may occur.

5 Once you're happy with your seam placement, make a small clip into the centre-front V, being careful not to cut through the stitch line, before unpicking any visible gathering stitches. Finish the raw edge on an overlocker (or use zigzag stitch) and press the seam allowance upwards.

6 Pin the back bodice pieces to the back skirt pieces, right sides together, and stitch in place. Finish the raw edges and press the seam allowance upwards.

7 Place the completed back pieces on top of the front piece, matching the shoulders seams. Pin in place and stitch. Finish the raw edges and press the seam allowance towards the back.

Adding the cap sleeves

8 Finish the bottom edge of the sleeves with a narrow rolled hem: press under 0.2cm (⅛in) and edgestitch it place. Press under 0.2cm (⅛in) again and stitch in place as before. Alternatively, you can use a rolled-hem foot to stitch this hem.

9 Run two rows of gathering stitches along the top of the sleeve (see my technique tutorial on gathering on page 64).

10 Match each edge of the cap sleeve to the notches on the main bodice, and the central notch to the shoulder seam. Use the gathering stitches to evenly distribute the ease around the top of the sleeve (this will be very minimal), pin in place and stitch. Unpick any visible gathering stitches remaining.

11 Place the front and back of your dress right sides together and pin the side seams, starting from the underarm edge and continuing all the way down to the hem, matching notches. Sew in place, taking care to avoid any stretching as you sew.

12 Now is a good time to try on your dress to check the overall fit (you will need to roughly pin the seam closed where the zip will eventually be inserted). Once happy with the fit, finish the raw edges and press towards the back. A good amount of steam will help to resolve any wavy seams.

Finishing the armholes

13 Roughly measure a strip of bias binding around each armhole and cut a length 2.5cm (1in) longer than required. Head over to page 100 if you want to make your own.

10

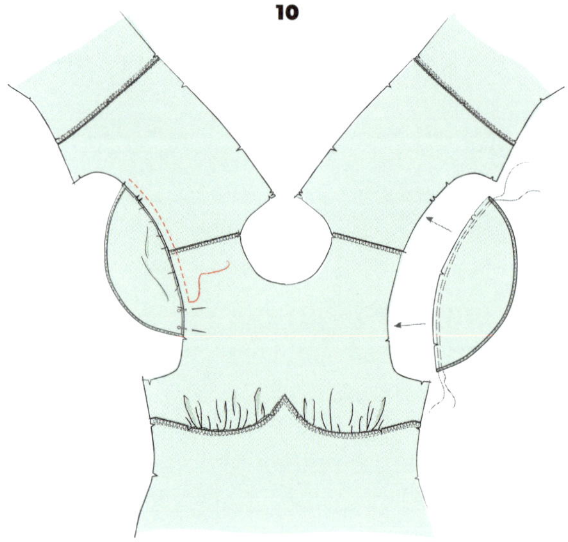

14 Please note that the way the armhole is finished with bias binding is a slightly different technique than usual, so please follow these instructions carefully. Starting where the edge of the cap sleeve joins to the armhole, open out your binding and, with right sides together, place the pressed crease in line with the 1cm (3⁄8in) seam allowance. Press under the binding end by about 0.5cm (1⁄4in) so no raw edges will be showing. Stitch all the way round the armhole along the seam line. Overlap the ends of binding by just over 0.5cm (1⁄4in) to ensure all raw edges will be hidden.

14

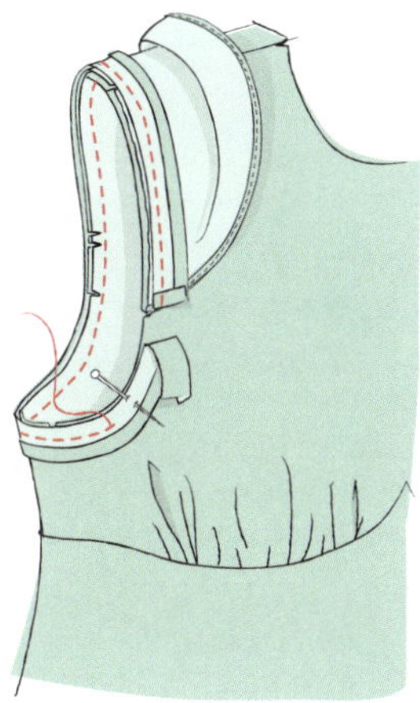

15 Trim the seam allowance down so it is now in line with the edge of the binding.

16 Gently use your fingers to press the binding over so it covers the raw edge and edgestitch in place, starting in line with the cap sleeve and finishing at the other end of the sleeve. Make sure to keep the sleeve out of the way as these stitches are purely to finish the raw edge and shouldn't be visible from the right side of the dress.

16

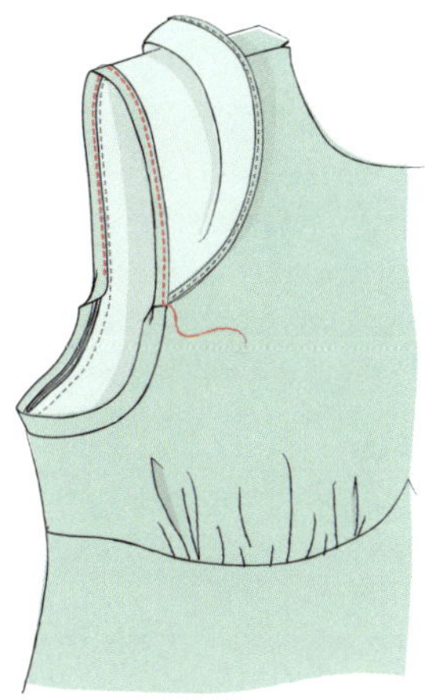

17 To finish the remaining part of the armhole, press the binding under towards the wrong side and pin in place. Stitch in place at 0.8cm (5⁄16in), tapering in your stitching slightly at each end to meet the previous stitch line in the cap-sleeve binding.

18 Finish with a good press with lots of steam to solve any stretching.

17

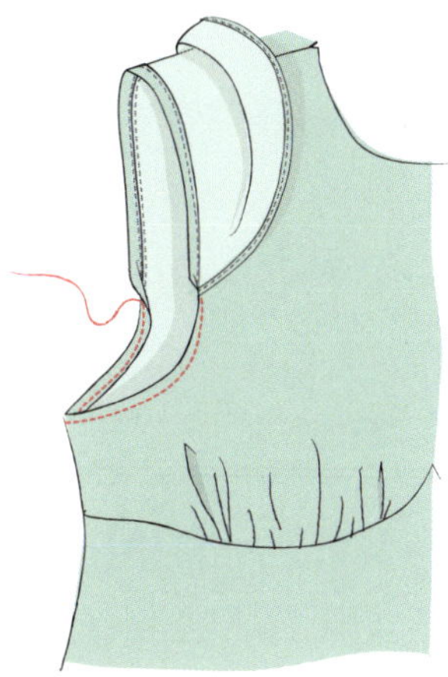

Adding the zip & finishing the neck

19 Use an overlocker or zigzag stitch to finish the raw edges at the centre back.

20 Insert the invisible zip following the detailed instructions in the technique tutorial on page 142. The bottom of the zip should line up with the zipper notch on the centre back and the raw edges should line up at the neckline.

21 Sew up the rest of the centre-back seam as close as possible to the bottom of the zip, and hand sew any remaining gap.

22 Taking a piece of your prepared bias binding, open it out and roughly pin it right sides together to the neck edge. The crease should line up with the line of stay stitching and you should have an excess of 1cm (⅜in) of binding on each end of the neckline. Sew in place.

23 Trim the seam allowance down so it's in line with the edge of the binding and press the binding to the wrong side of the neckline so no binding is visible from the right side. You also need to press under each of the short ends, so the excess is hidden within the binding. Stitch in place at just under 1cm (⅜in), taking care not to let the fabric pucker as you sew.

24 Give the neckline a good press with lots of steam.

20

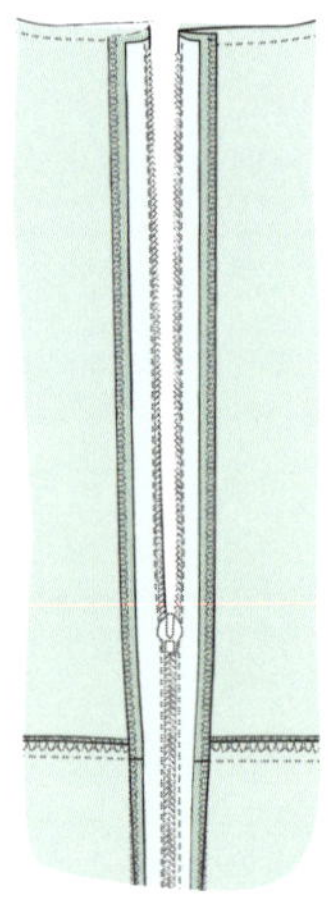

22

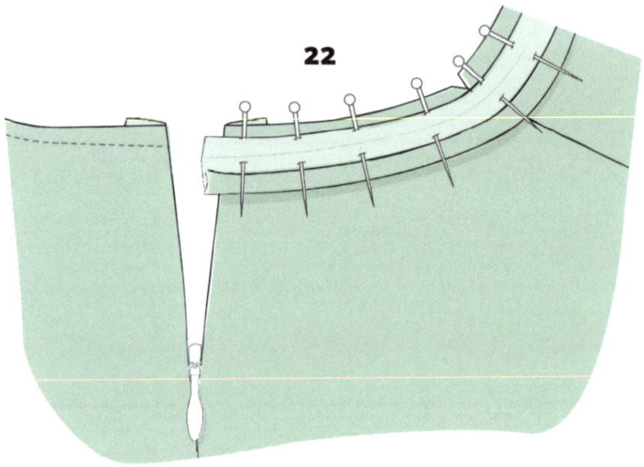

Finishing touches

25 Hand sew a small hook-and-eye to the very top of the neckline above the zip to keep it fully closed.

26 If desired, you can hand sew a small ready-made bow to the centre-front neckline of your dress for a cute extra touch.

27 It's always wise to hang a bias-cut garment for a few days before hemming it, as the fabric often stretches out. Once you've done that, try it on to check you are happy with the length and trim off any wavy sections of the hemline if needed.

28 Create a narrow rolled hem as you did for the sleeves (see step 8).

Woo! The Tea Dress is complete, and you are ready to go to your lunch date looking like you're straight off the catwalk! Why not throw on a leather jacket for a more off-duty look?

Styling suggestion

Don't just save your dress for special occasions! One of my favourite ways to style the Tea Dress is to layer it with a cosy knit and pair it with some comfy trainers for a more casual look. People will think you're wearing a cute bias-cut skirt. See pages 182–183 for more cute year-round styling suggestions.

VARIATION

Bias-cut top

It's a bold statement, but this could be one of my favourite designs, so I couldn't resist making a top version too. This is the same silhouette as the dress, but can easily be styled with jeans or even a slip skirt. Your fabric choice makes all the difference here – you can use the same fabric for all of your pattern pieces, or play around with a pattern clash like I did for my dress. If you're unsure, try sketching out your ideas and colour combinations before making your final decision.

Finished length measurements

	6	8	10	12	14	16	18	20	22
Front length (cm)	54.8	55.4	56	56.6	57.2	59.2	60.8	61.9	62
Front length (in)	21½	21¾	22	22¼	22½	23¼	24	24¼	24½

Fabric requirements

- Sizes 6–14: 1.25m (1½yd) of fabric, 150cm (60in) wide
  Sizes 16–22: 1.5m (1¾yd) of fabric, 150cm (60in) wide
- For additional notions required, see page 68

Making the variation

1 Cut out your pattern pieces, making sure to choose the top option for the lower front and back bodice.

2 Follow the instructions for making the dress, ignoring any references to the front and back skirt pieces (we will use our lower front and back bodice here instead).

3 As with the dress, you should hang your top for a few days before hemming to allow the bias-cut fabric to find its own form.

Top tip!

This top is yours to make your own – I love the look of the bow at the neckline, but you could even play around with adding some small buttons to the centre front instead.

Cutting guide

1 Bodice front – cut 1 on fold

2 Bodice back – cut 2

3 Skirt front – cut 1 on fold

4 Skirt back – cut 2

5 Sleeve – cut 2

6 Armhole binding – cut 2

7 Neckline binding – cut 1

All sizes: 150cm (60in) wide fabric

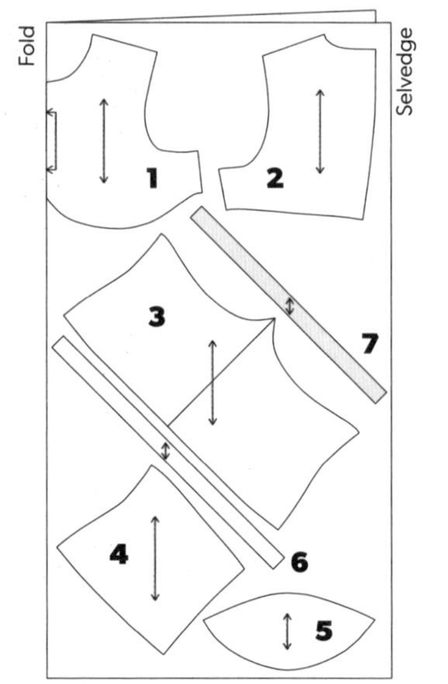

Technique Tutorial: *Cutting & sewing on the bias*

Rotary cutter

Working on the bias means cutting the fabric at a 45-degree angle to the fabric grain rather than following the straight weave. This gives the fabric a more elastic stretch and creates a dreamy drape that will hug your body perfectly. For newer sewers, working on the bias can seem daunting, as it can be easy to stretch out the seams or have an uneven hem, so I've rounded up my top tips for sewing on the bias to enable you to get into this project with confidence!

Cutting out

- If you generally use scissors to cut out, try opting for a sharp rotary cutter instead. The rotary cutter will slice through the fabric and reduce the amount of pulling and movement, which is particularly common with slippery fabrics like satin.

Ballpoint needle

- Handle your fabric with care! It might sound silly, but simple things like dangling your fabric off a table edge can encourage bias-cut pieces to stretch out. Try to handle your fabrics as little as possible and keep them flat on a surface when not in use.

Sewing

- Switch to an extra-sharp or ballpoint needle. This will pierce the fabric more easily and give a neater finish to your seams.

- Stay stitching will be your best friend when it comes to bias-cut fabrics. Stay stitch any neckline edges and other bias-cut edges that may stretch out by sewing a line of stitches on or just within the seam allowance.
- Use lots of pins! Pinning your fabric in place across the whole length of a seam will reduce any stretching that may take place. Start by matching the fabric edges and any notches before easing in the rest of the seam.
- Support your fabric as you sew to avoid stretching. Don't let your fabric dangle off the edge of the sewing-machine table: make sure it is well supported and being held up as you sew.
- If you think your fabric is stretching out as it goes through the machine, try reducing your presser-foot pressure, or switch to a walking foot which will feed the fabric through more evenly.

Finishing touches

- It can be tempting to rush to finish a garment, but for bias-cut dresses, it's essential you hang it up for at least a day before hemming. More often than not, gravity will do its thing and you'll end up with a wavy hem as the warp and weft threads stretch out. This kind of stretching is pretty inevitable, so let it hang before going in and evening up the hem prior to sewing.
- Don't forget about steam! I've already spoken about the magical powers of steam when sewing with stretch fabrics, and you'll be pleased to know it can also be a lifesaver when it comes to bias-cut garments too. If your seams are looking a bit wavy, give them a good press with lots of steam and watch the stretching disappear! (Do bear in mind that you may need to reduce your iron temperature depending on what fabric you are using, so you may want to test the settings on a piece of scrap fabric first. We don't want any singed satin.)

Top tip!

Now you're ready to tackle sewing on the bias. If it's your first time, you may want to consider sewing a toile dress first, not only to check the fit, but also to give you the opportunity to practise these techniques without ruining costly fabric!

THE BUFFET DRESS

Ruffle collar, mini-length, button closure

All my wildest dress dreams came true in this design! I've always been a fan of a statement collar, but add in a loose-fit buffet-style bodice and I'm head over heels. I think this is one of the most versatile projects in the book: leave the collar off for a simpler design, go wild with a textured bouclé fabric to create a layering piece, or try out an all-over gingham for a cutesy summer dress. I can't wait to see my social feed filled with your Buffet Dresses!

Fabric suggestions

As long as it's woven, chances are the fabric will work for this dress! Think about how dressy or casual you want your finished piece to be to help you make the perfect choice. Try:

- Cotton/polycotton
- Brocade/jacquard
- Bouclé/tweed

Notions

- 2m (2¼yd) of main fabric, 150cm (60in) wide
- 1m (1yd) of fabric for the collar, 150cm (60in) wide
- 0.6m (¾yd) of light- to medium-weight iron-on woven interfacing of a similar weight to your chosen fabric
- Five 1–2cm (⅜–¾in) buttons, depending on your desired look
- Handmade or ready-made bias binding, 1.5cm (⅝in) wide (see page 100 to make your own)

Top tip!

When using fabrics with directional prints – especially large, obvious patterns – you may need extra fabric so you can arrange your pattern pieces on the fabric to get the best out of your print.

Notes

- All seams should be sewn with a 1cm (⅜in) seam allowance unless otherwise stated.
- Check out my technique tutorials on gathering (page 64), bias binding (page 100) and buttonholes (page 162) before you begin.
- Conversions to imperial measurements aren't always precise as they often need to be rounded up or down, but they do work with the patterns. Stick with either the metric or imperial measurements – don't mix and match.

Finished measurements

	6	8	10	12	14	16	18	20	22
Bust (cm)	91	96	101	106	111	116	121	126	131
Bust (in)	36	37¾	39¾	41¾	43¾	45½	47½	49½	51½
Waist (cm)	88.6	93.6	98.6	103.6	108.6	113.6	118.6	123.6	128.6
Waist (in)	34¾	36¾	38¾	40¾	42¾	44¾	46¾	48½	50½
Front hem width (cm)	91.3	93.8	96.3	98.8	101.3	103.8	106.3	108.8	111.3
Front hem width (in)	36	37	38	39	39¾	40¾	41¾	42¾	43¾
Front length (cm)	89.8	90.4	91	91.6	92.2	92.8	93.4	94	94.6
Front length (in)	35¼	35½	3	36	36¼	36½	36¾	37	37¼
Collar length (cm)	11.5	11.5	11.5	11.5	11.5	11.5	11.5	11.5	11.5
Collar length (in)	4½	4½	4½	4½	4½	4½	4½	4½	4½

Cutting guide

1 Bodice front – cut 1 on fold

2 Bodice back – cut 2

3 Neckline facing – cut 1 main fabric and 1 interfacing

4 Skirt front – cut 1 on fold

5 Skirt back – cut 1 on fold

6 Collar – cut 4 main fabric and 2 interfacing

7 Collar ruffle – cut 2

8 Bias binding template – cut 2 on the bias (see page 82)

9 Placket interfacing – cut 2 interfacing

All sizes: 150cm (60in) wide main fabric

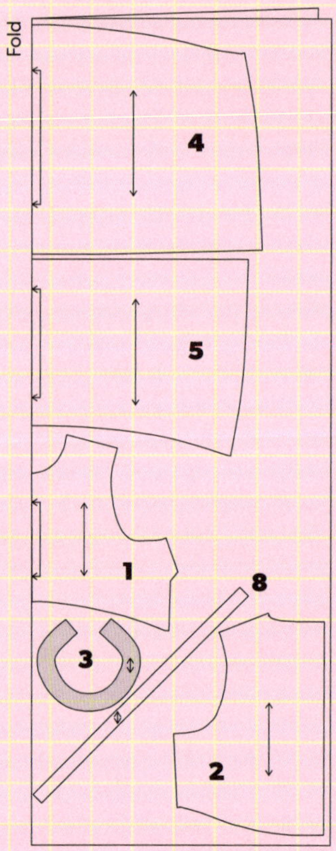

All sizes: 150cm (60in) wide collar fabric

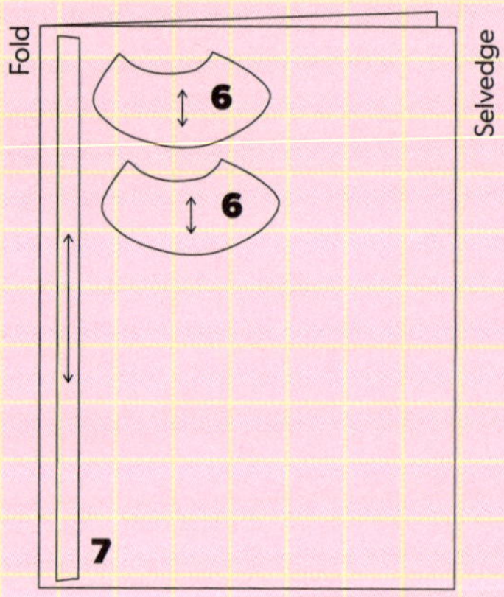

Interfacing

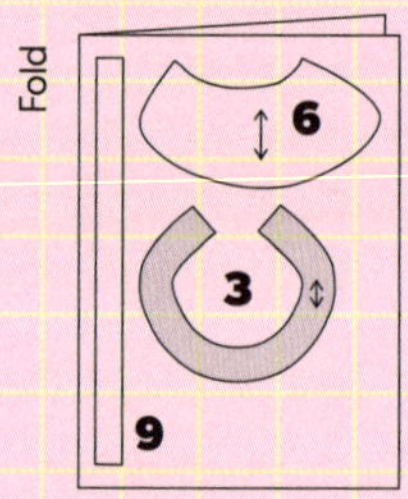

Constructing the bodice

1 Cut out the fabric pieces and transfer markings, including the bodice darts. Iron fusible interfacing onto one left and one right collar piece.

2 With right sides together, fold your fabric and sew along the dart markings you transferred. Leave a tail of thread at the point of each dart and tie a knot to finish. Press the darts down towards the waistline.

3 Pin the bodice front and back together at the shoulder and side seams. Stitch these seams, overlock (or zigzag) the raw edges and press the seam allowances towards the back.

2

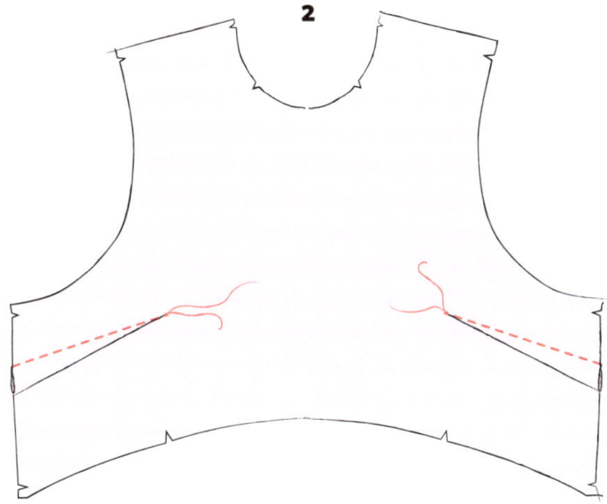

Making the ruffle collar

4 Take each collar ruffle piece, press under 0.2cm (⅛in) along one of the long edges (the bottom edge) and then press under 0.2cm (⅛in) again. Topstitch in place.

4

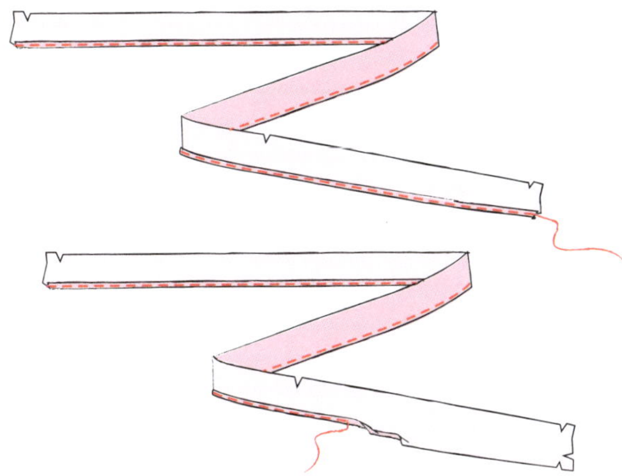

5 Run two rows of gathering stitches along the remaining long edge (see my technique tutorial on gathering on page 64). Gently pull on the gathering stitches to gather the collar ruffle to be the same size as the outer edge of both outer collar pieces (the uninterfaced pieces) and pin in place. Baste to the collar at just under 1cm (⅜in).

5

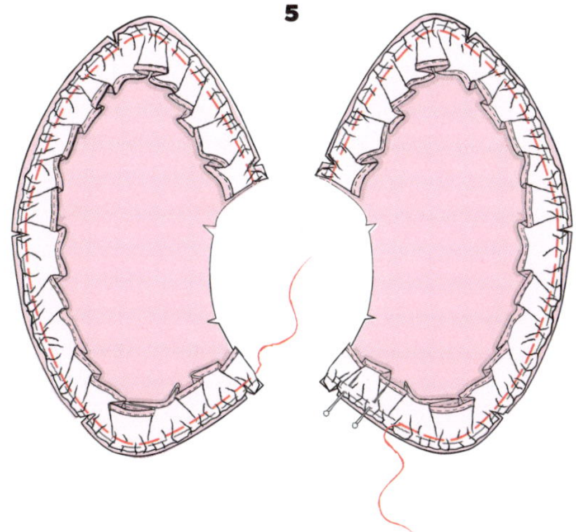

6 Place the corresponding interfaced collar piece directly on top, with right sides together, and stitch in place, making sure the gathers remain even on the ruffle piece.

7 Clip the curves and turn each collar right side out. Press well before topstitching all the way round the collar at about 0.2cm (⅛in) away from the frill.

8 Pin both collar pieces to the neckline edges with the right side facing up, matching notches. The interfaced piece should be facing down and the edge of the frills should meet at the centre front. Baste in place at just under 1cm (3⁄8in).

Finishing the bodice

9 Overlock (or zigzag) the outside edge of the neckline facing, then press under 0.5cm (1⁄4in) and topstitch in place.

10 Pin the facing to the neckline with right sides together. The collar will be sandwiched between the bodice and the facing. Stitch in place then understitch and press towards the inside of the dress. (See page 178 for instructions on understitching.)

11 With the right side facing up and the facing pressed to the inside of the bodice, topstitch around the neckline 1cm (3⁄8in) away from the seam edge to keep the facing in place. Make sure the collar is tucked up and out of the way, so you are only sewing through the bodice and facing.

12 Press under 1cm (3⁄8in) along each of the long placket edges.

8

9

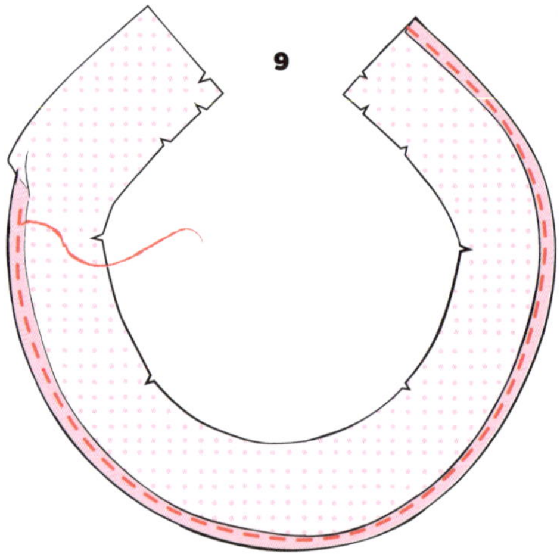

10

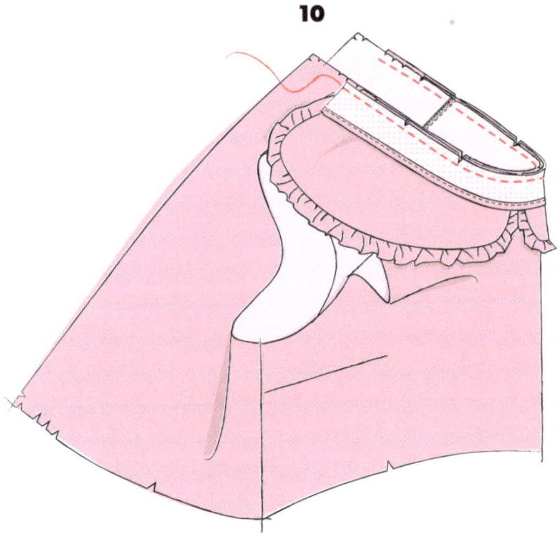

13 Fold the placket back on itself with right sides together, making sure the 1cm (⅜in) edge is still pressed under. Sew a 1cm (⅜in) seam at the top of the placket, along the short edge. Clip the seam allowance at the corner and turn out. This will finish the remaining top edge of the dress.

14 Now press the placket along the fold line, which will leave a 2.5cm (1in) strip. Topstitch it in place.

15 Following the markings transferred from the pattern piece, sew seven buttonholes down the centre of the placket (see page 162). Traditionally, the buttonholes should be on the left-hand side of the back bodice.

16 Once you're happy with the buttonholes, trim the threads, cut out the centre of each one and then hand stitch your buttons to the opposite side of the placket to correspond.

17 Place the bottom of the left-hand side placket (with the buttonholes) over the right-hand side, so the placket overlaps, and baste in place.

13

17

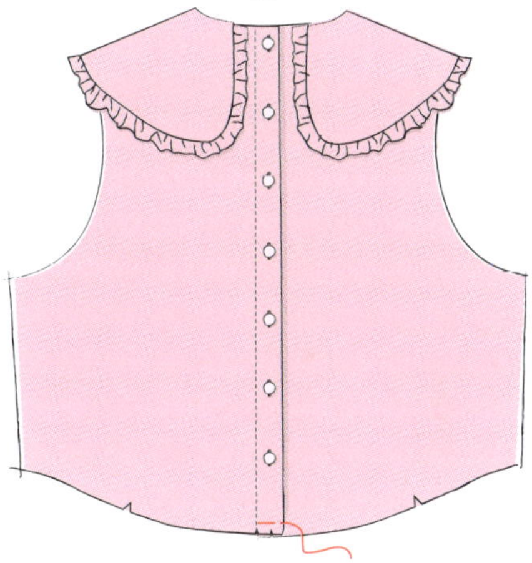

Finishing the armholes

18 Now you'll need your strips of bias binding to finish the armhole. Head over to page 100 if you want to make your own. Roughly measure a strip of bias binding around each armhole and cut a length 2.5cm (1in) longer than required.

19 Go to page 102 of my technique tutorial on bias binding to see how to attach your binding to the armhole and give it a neat finish.

Attaching the skirt

20 Place the skirt front and back right sides together at the side seams, matching notches. Stitch these seams in place. Finish the raw edges and press to the back.

21 Sew two lines of gathering stitches along the waistline edge of the skirt (see my technique tutorial on gathering on page 64).

22 Pin the skirt and bodice waistline together at the side seams, making sure they match exactly. Gently pull on the gathering stitches until the skirt is the same width as the bodice waistline. Pin in place and stitch.

23 Finish the raw edges of the seam allowances and press up towards the bodice.

Finishing touches

24 Try on your dress to make sure you're happy with the length and make any adjustments necessary.

25 To hem the dress, press under 0.5cm (¼in) and then a further 1.5cm (⅝in). Topstitch in place.

Woo!

And just like that, your buffet dress is complete! I just know this is going to become a staple in your wardrobe and it can be styled in so many ways. Don't be afraid to play around with layering underneath to create some fun outfit combinations.

Styling suggestion

This dress is made to be layered for different seasons! If you're anything like me, you'll already have a few blouses with statement collars in your wardrobe. Try popping them on under your dress to play around with some different looks. For some seasonal looks, see pages 184–185.

VARIATION

No collar, knee-length

I love the flamboyance of a frilly collar, but I also like to have the option of a simpler design in my wardrobe, too. By leaving off the collar, you'll give the Buffet Dress a radically different look that is perfect for layering knitwear underneath. I also included the option of a knee-length skirt with a slightly curved waistline, which is suitable for those colder months and balances perfectly with the simple neckline.

Finished length measurements

	6	8	10	12	14	16	18	20	22
Front length (cm)	107.8	108.4	109	109.6	110.2	110.8	111.4	112	112.6
Front length (in)	42½	42⅝	43	43¼	43½	43⅝	43¾	44	44¼

Fabric requirements

- Sizes 6–14: 2m (2¼yd) of main fabric, 150cm (60in) wide
  Sizes 16–22: 2.4m (2¾yd) of main fabric, 150cm (60in) wide
- For additional notions required, see page 86

Making the variation

1 Cut out your pattern pieces, making sure to choose the knee-length skirt pieces.

2 Follow the instructions for the dress, skipping over the section for making the ruffle collar, then finish the armholes and attach the skirt as normal.

3 As always, try on your dress before hemming, as this is the time to make any final adjustments to the length.

Top tip!

Your fabric choice will have a big effect on the final look of this dress – a brocade like I used in this variation will create a statement, full-bodied skirt, whereas opting for a viscose would give the dress a lot more drape.

Cutting guide

1 Bodice front – cut 1 on fold

2 Bodice back – cut 2

3 Neckline facing – cut 1 main fabric and 1 interfacing

4 Skirt front – cut 1 on fold

5 Skirt back – cut 1 on fold

6 Bias binding template – cut 2 on the bias (see page 82)

7 Placket interfacing – cut 2 interfacing

All sizes: 150cm (60in) wide main fabric

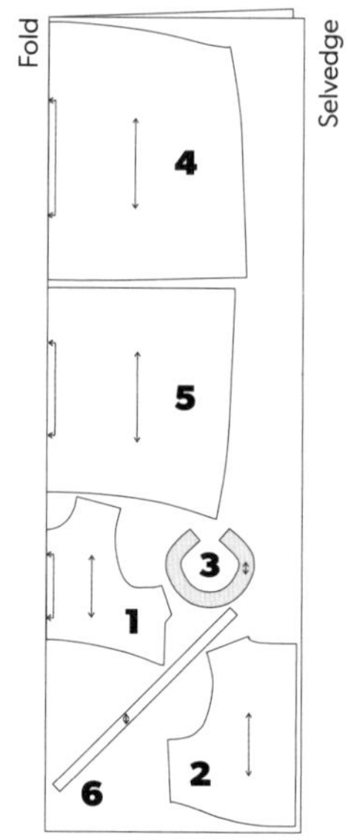

Interfacing

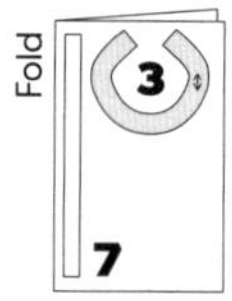

Technique Tutorial: *Bias binding*

Bias binding is commonly used in garments to finish necklines and armholes in place of a facing or lining. The bias cut helps the binding to stretch around the curved edges and finish them in a professional way. When I'm short on time, I often prefer to use ready-made binding, but for projects like the Buffet Dress, when I want the binding to match perfectly, it's always a good idea to make your own.

I'll start by taking you through the steps to make your own binding, and then on pages 102–103 you can see how to attach your binding – whether its me-made or ready-made – to an armhole. If you want to use your binding to finish a neckline, the process is pretty much the same.

Note that although you can cut binding strips with scissors, it's much quicker and more precise with a rotary cutter and cutting mat.

Making your own binding

1 Take your fabric and fold it in half on the bias (at a 45-degree angle).

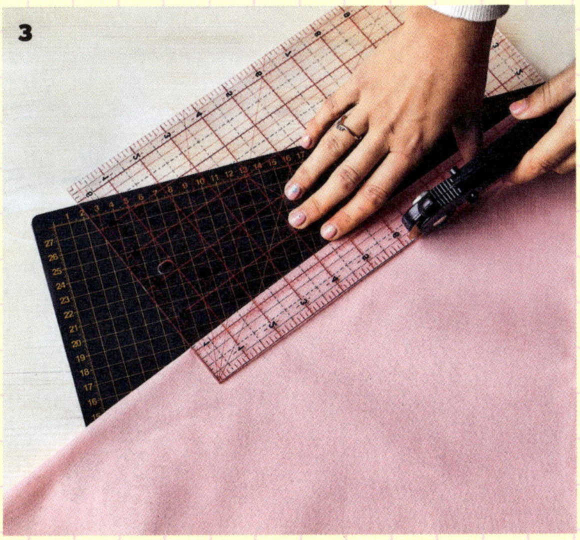

2 Use a ruler to draw strips parallel to this fold (if you are using a rotary cutter, you can skip this step once you get the hang of it). The width of the strips will be determined by the width of the bias binding required. For the Buffet Dress, we will be using 1.5cm (⅝in) wide binding, so your strips should measure 3cm (1¼in) wide.

3 Cut out your strips. I prefer to use a rotary cutter for this method and cut against my ruler to ensure the strips are completely straight.

4 The short end of each strip also needs to be cut completely straight to allow us to join the strips together accurately.

5 With right sides facing, pin the short ends together to create a right angle. Now sew the two strips together diagonally from one edge to the other.

6 Once sewn, trim the seam allowances down to 1cm (⅜in), and press open. When unfolded, the strips will align perfectly in a long piece of binding.

7 To finish the binding, we need to press under 0.7cm (5⁄16in) along each of the long edges. This can be hard to do accurately by hand, so I often like to opt for a bias-binding maker. For this option, feed the strip through the open end of the binding maker with the wrong side facing upwards. Holding one end of the strip, gently pull the binding maker along the fabric. Use a hot iron to press this in place as you pull. You will see some perfectly pressed binding beginning to form!

Top tip!

Binding makers come in different sizes and are available in handy sets. Your bias-cut fabric strips need to be around twice the width of the binding maker, so for a 1.5cm (⅝in) binding maker your strips should be 3cm (1¼in) wide.

Attaching the binding

1 The method of attaching binding can vary depending on the project, so please read the pattern instructions carefully. This method is correct for finishing the armholes of the Buffet Dress.

2 Fold under the short end of the binding by 1cm (3⁄8in) and, starting at the underarm seam, pin it in place with the folded end 1.5cm (5⁄8in) before the seam. The crease in the binding should be lined up with the seam allowance on the bodice. Continue to pin the binding all the way round the rest of the armhole with right sides together.

3

3 Stitch the binding in place along the binding fold. You don't want to overly stretch the binding as you sew but you do want it to be held taut to the fabric to give a close fit. Continue sewing right up to the underarm seam, so your binding ends overlap by 1.5cm (5⁄8in).

4 Carefully clip into the curves of the armhole without cutting through the stitch line.

5 Using a hot and steamy iron, press the seam allowance up towards the binding.

6 Now press the full binding towards the wrong side of the armhole. The folded edge should be hidden underneath so no raw edges are showing. Pin in place. If you need to trim the seam allowances slightly, go ahead and do so.

7

7 Edgestitch the binding in place close to the outer edge. It can be easy to get little tucks or puckers in the main fabric around the armhole, so take your time as you sew.

8 Give the whole armhole a final press, using lots of steam if there's been any stretching or puckering.

Woo!

Now step back and admire the beautiful armholes! The bound finish not only looks smart, but the armholes will feel comfortable, too, because there are no rough seam edges on the inside of the dress that might rub.

THE EVERYDAY DRESS

Shirred bodice, short puff sleeve, tiered mini skirt

This certainly wouldn't be a book of my dream dresses without a serious amount of shirring. If you've followed along with my sewing journey for a while, you will be familiar with my love of the classic shirred dress made of rectangles. I already have a highly popular free tutorial for this on my YouTube channel, so of course for the book I wanted to bring you some shirring with a twist... Queue the fully shirred bodice! Now this may look daunting, but by shirring panels of fabric prior to cutting out the bodice, it actually couldn't be easier. So, grab those elastic reels and let's get shirring...

Fabric suggestions

Light- to medium-weight woven fabrics are what work best for this dress. It's also worth keeping in mind how you want the shirring to look: lighter weight fabrics will create a tighter shirring, whereas medium-weight fabrics may produce slightly less of a gather. Try to avoid anything too heavy as it will be difficult to shir and may lead to a poor-fitting bodice. Try:

- Cotton/polycotton
- Viscose
- Linen

Notions

- Sizes 6–14: 2m (2¼yd) of main fabric, 150cm (60in) wide. Sizes 16–22: 2.3m (2½yd) of main fabric, 150cm (60in) wide
- Shirring elastic (and lots of it!)
- 1cm (⅜in) wide elastic for the cuffs
- 2.5cm (1in) wide elastic for the waistband

Notes

- All seams should be sewn with a 1cm (⅜in) seam allowance unless otherwise stated.
- Check out my technique tutorials on gathering (page 64) and shirring (page 122) before you begin.
- Conversions to imperial measurements aren't always precise as they often need to be rounded up or down, but they do work with the patterns. Stick with either the metric or imperial measurements – don't mix and match.

Finished measurements

	6	8	10	12	14	16	18	20	22
Bust (cm)	76	81	86	91	96	101	106	111	116
Bust (in)	30	31¾	34	36	37¾	39¾	41¾	43¾	45½
Waist (cm)	63.4	68.4	73.4	78.4	83.4	88.4	93.4	98.4	103.4
Waist (in)	25	27	29	31	33	34¾	36¾	38¾	40¾
Front hem width (cm)	101	103.5	106	108.5	111	113.5	116	118.5	121
Front hem width (in)	39¾	40¾	41¾	42¾	43¾	44¾	45½	46¾	47½
Front length (cm)	88	88.6	89.2	89.8	90.4	91	91.6	92.2	92.8
Front length (in)	34½	34¾	35	35¼	35½	35¾	36	36¼	36½
Sleeve length (cm)	28.8	29.3	29.8	30.3	30.8	31.3	31.8	32.3	32.8
Sleeve length (in)	11¼	11½	11¾	12	12¼	12³/₈	12½	12¾	13

Elastic length

	6	8	10	12	14	16	18	20	22
Short sleeve (cm)	24	25.6	27.2	28.8	30.4	32	33.6	35.2	36.8
Short sleeve (in)	9½	10	10¾	11¼	12	12½	13¼	14	14½
Long sleeve (cm)	16	16.8	17.6	18.4	19.2	20	20.8	21.6	22.4
Long sleeve (in)	6¼	6½	7	7¼	7½	8	8¼	8½	8¾
Waist (cm)	62.7	67.7	72.7	77.7	82.7	87.7	92.7	97.7	102.7
Waist (in)	24½	26½	28½	30½	32½	34½	36½	38½	40½

Cutting guide

1 Shirred panel – cut 2

2 Bodice front – cut 1 on fold on shirred fabric

3 Bodice back – cut 1 on fold on shirred fabric

4 Short sleeve – cut 2

5 Collar frill – cut 1

6 Front skirt upper tier – cut 1 on fold

7 Back skirt upper tier – cut 1 on fold

8 Front skirt lower tier – cut 1 on fold

9 Back skirt lower tier – cut 1 on fold

10 Front waistband – cut 1 on fold

11 Back waistband – cut 1 on fold

12 Waist tie – cut 2

All sizes: shirred panels

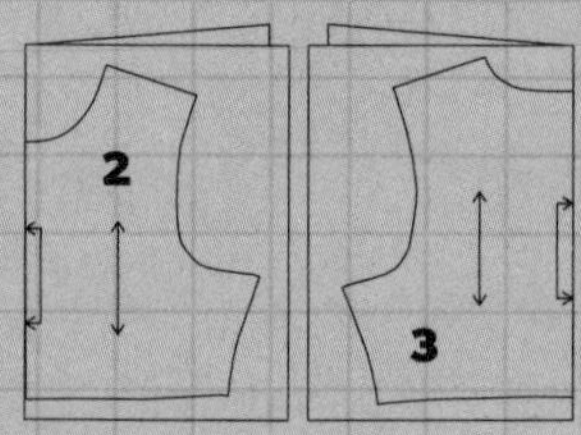

Sizes 6–14: 150cm (60in) wide fabric

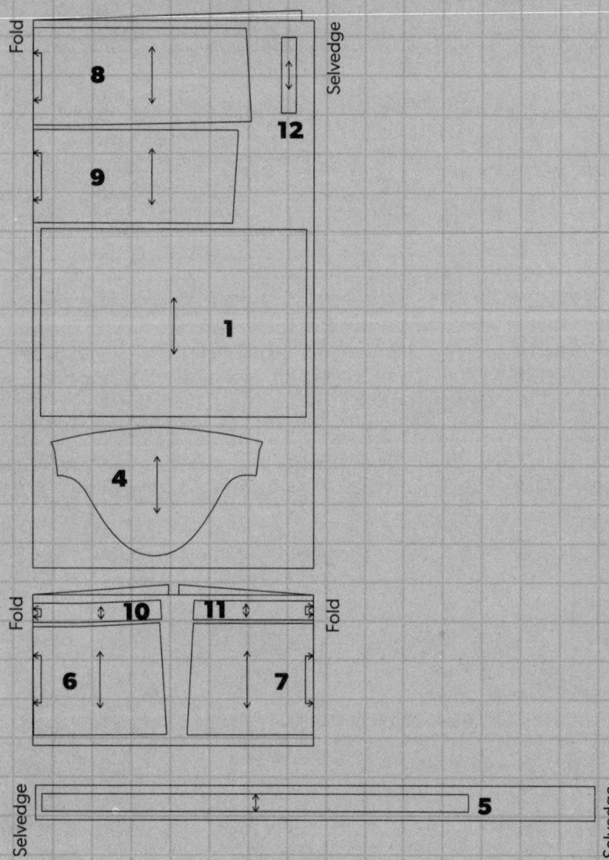

Sizes 16–22: 150cm (60in) wide fabric

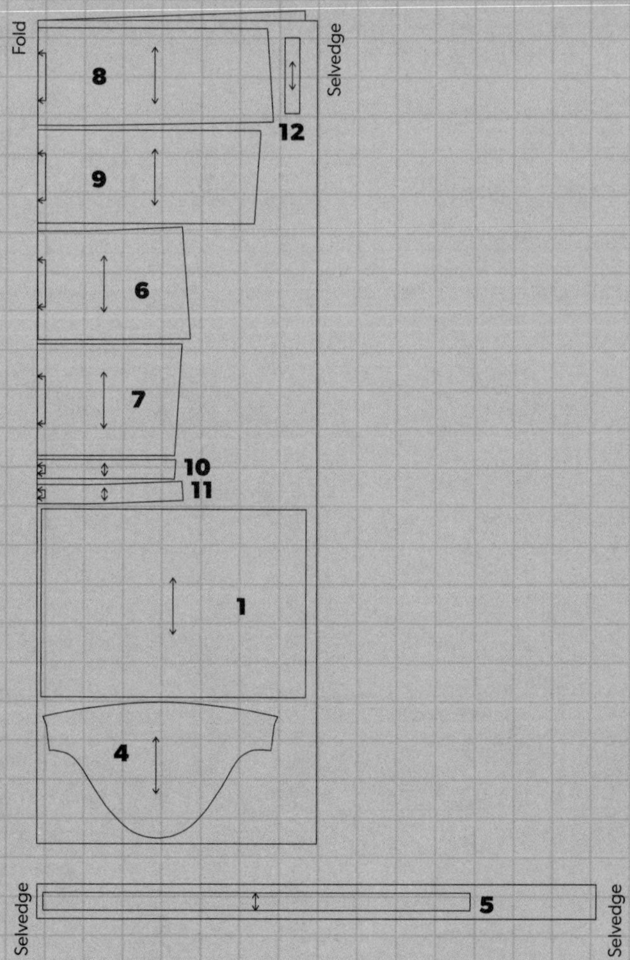

Pattern prep

1 Cut out all your pattern pieces from your main fabric except for the bodice front and back. We will need to shir the panels before cutting these out directly from the shirred fabric. It's worth bearing in mind that all fabrics will gather in by varying amounts, so it's a good idea to test the level of gathering and make your panels wider if necessary to allow for enough fabric.

2 Following the lines on the pattern, sew your lines of shirring, starting and ending where the notches indicate. Make sure to use my shirring technique tutorial (page 122) to help you!

3 Once the panels are shirred, cut out your bodice front and back as normal on the fold. Don't try to stretch the fabric as you do so. You may find it easier to use a rotary cutter and self-healing mat to do this.

Top tip! The shirring process can be fairly time-consuming, so pop on your favourite show, grab a cuppa and enjoy some mindful sewing!

3

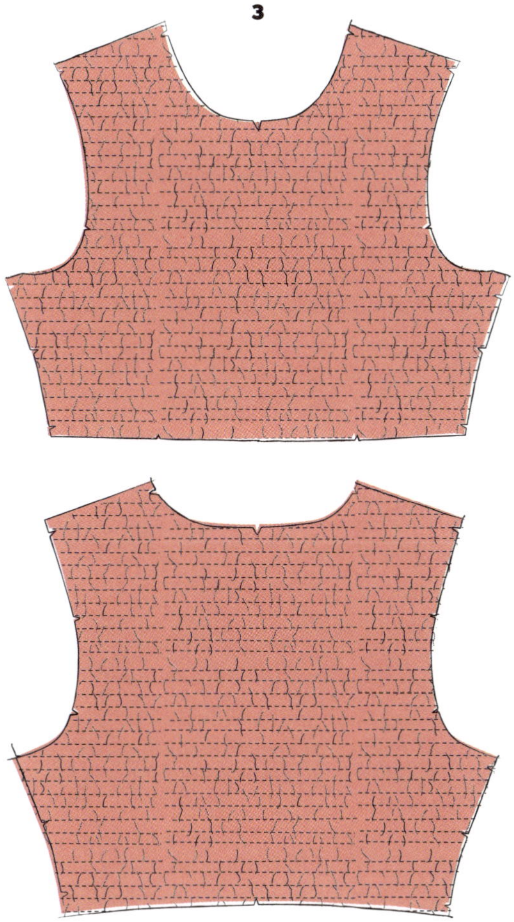

Constructing the bodice

4 With right sides together, place your bodice front and back together and pin in place at the shoulder and side seams. Sew in place and then finish the raw edges on an overlocker (or with zigzag stitch).

5 Take your neckline frill and fold it in half so that the short ends are right sides together. Pin and stitch in place. Finish the raw edges using your chosen method and press the seam open.

6 Finish one long edge of the neckline frill (the bottom edge) with a narrow hem by pressing under 0.2cm (⅛in), edgestitching in place and repeating a second time.

7 Along the remaining long edge, sew two rows of gathering stitches (see my technique tutorial on gathering on page 64).

8 Match the seam in the frill to one of the bodice shoulder seams and pin in place. Identify the centre-front and centre-back notches, match them to the frill piece and pin the frill in place. Gently pull on the gathering stitches to gather in the rest of the frill to fit the neckline, using plenty of pins to hold it securely.

9 When stitching this frill in place, we still want the neckline to have an element of stretch. Instead of using normal thread on the bobbin, wind it with shirring elastic. Sew the frill on using your normal stitch settings. Rather than shirring the neckline, it will attach the frill while keeping an element of elasticity.

10 Overlock (or zigzag) the raw edges together at the neckline without trimming off any excess. Press this finished seam down into the bodice and away from the neckline. With the right side of the bodice facing up, stitch the seam allowance down just under 1cm (⅜in) away from the neckline seam. Press the frill upwards.

5

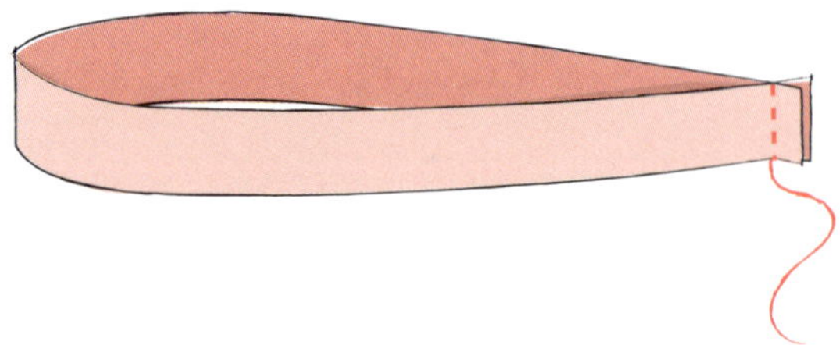

6

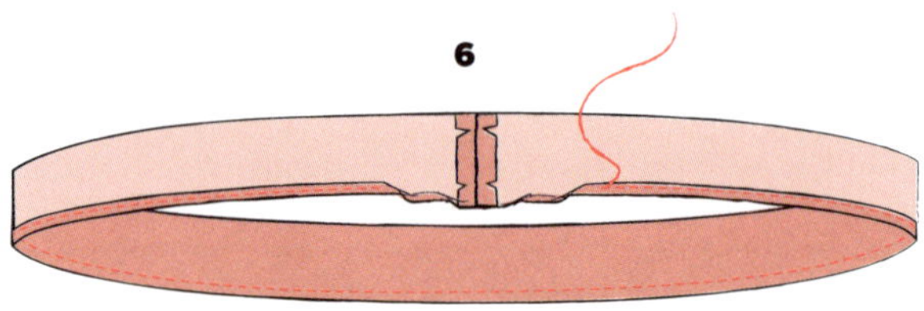

8

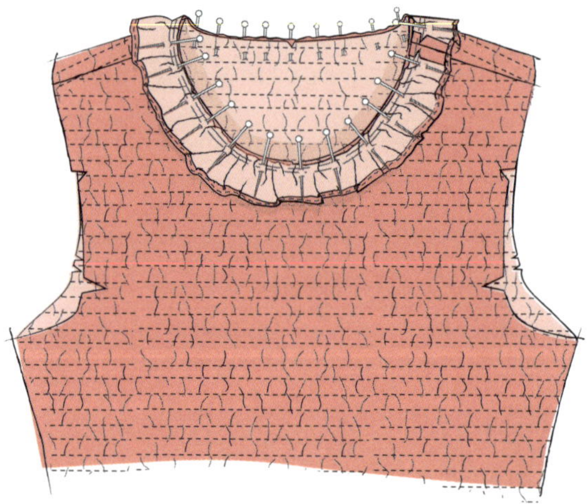

Adding the sleeves

11 Fold each sleeve in half to match the underarm seam, right sides together. Sew the seam, finish the raw edges and press the seam allowance towards the back.

12 Along the bottom edge of the sleeve, press under 1cm (⅜in) then press under a further 1.5cm (⅝in), this time following the notch in the sleeve edge. Pin and edgestitch in place, making sure to leave a 2.5cm (1in) opening so that you can feed the elastic through. (This will be added later, after inserting the sleeve.)

12

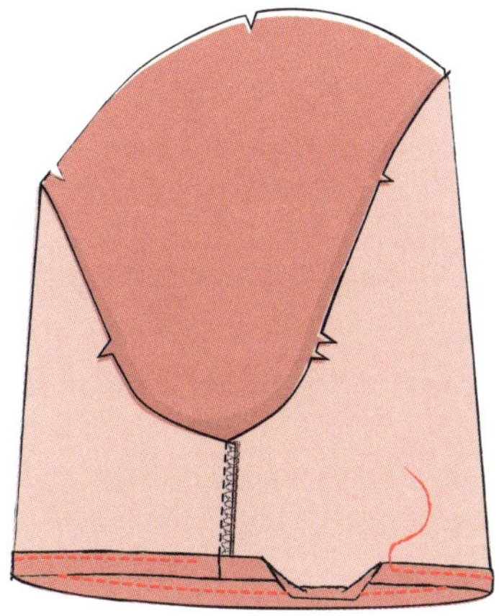

13 Sew two rows of gathering stitches between the notches on the sleeve head (see my technique tutorial on gathering on page 64).

14 To insert each sleeve, begin by matching the underarm seams of your bodice and sleeve with right sides together. Pin in place and continue round the sleeve, matching notches, until you reach the gathering notches. Gently pull on the gathers to evenly distribute them throughout the sleeve head and pin in place.

14

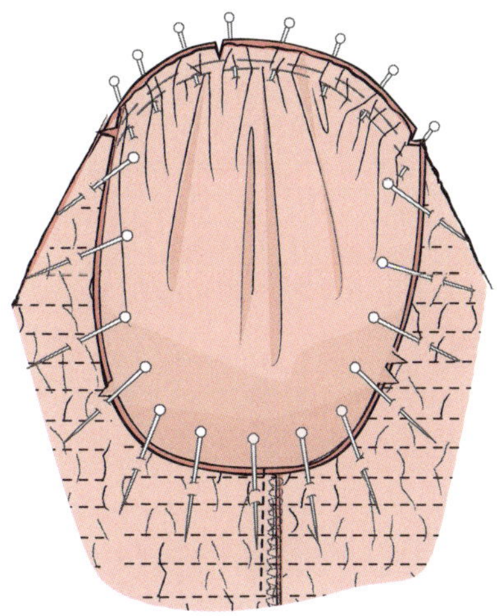

15 Sew the sleeve seam, finish the raw edges on the overlocker and press the seam allowance up into the sleeve.

16 Cut your sleeve elastic according to the pattern measurement and roughly check you're happy with the length. Adjust as necessary before using a safety pin to feed the elastic evenly through the channel.

17 Sew the short ends together with a regular 1cm (⅜in) seam allowance before edgestitching the remaining gap closed.

Preparing the skirt

18

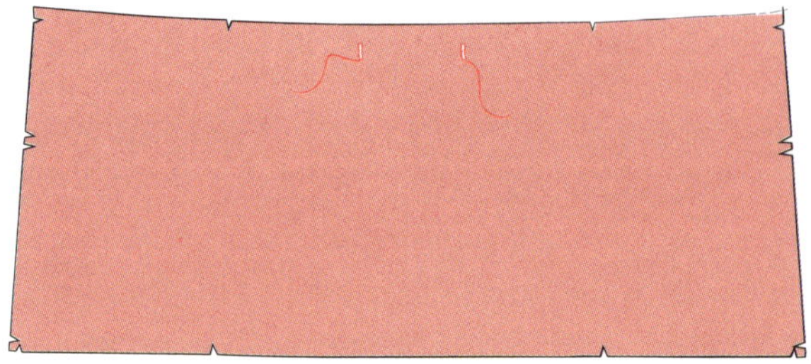

18 Following the pattern markings, use your buttonhole foot to sew the two buttonholes to the front skirt. Snip the centre and trim off any loose threads. Check out the technique tutorial on buttonholes (page 162) for extra help if needed.

19 Taking the pieces for the upper tier of the skirt, pin them with right sides facing at the side seams. Stitch the seams, finish the raw edges with your overlocker (or zigzag stitch) and press the seam allowances towards the back.

20 Repeat for the lower skirt tier.

21 On the top edge of the lower skirt tier, sew two rows of gathering stitches (see page 64).

22 Pin the lower tier to the upper skirt with right sides together, first matching the side seams and then the notches. Gently pull on the gathering stitches to gather the skirt edges to the same length. Pin and stitch in place. Finish the raw edge with an overlocker (or zigzag stitch) and press the seam allowance upwards.

Attaching the skirt & waistband

25

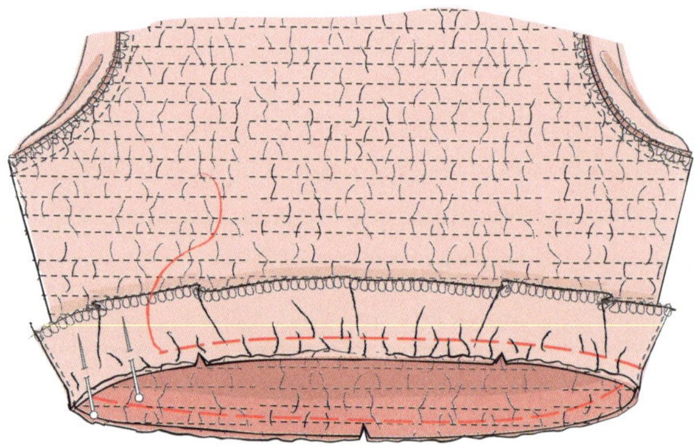

23 With right sides together, sew the side seams of the front and back waistbands. Finish the raw edges and press towards the back.

24 Now finish the lower raw edge of the waistband piece on the overlocker, avoiding trimming any of the fabric.

25 The separate waistband piece will form the inner waistband channel. Pin the right-side upper edge of the waistband to the wrong side of the bodice. Baste in place at 0.8cm (5⁄16in), stretching the shirred bodice as you sew.

26 Now, with right sides together, pin the skirt to the bodice at the waistline, matching the notches and side seams. Sew the skirt to the bodice with a regular seam allowance. Make sure the inner waistband is laying flat underneath as we will be stitching through all layers. You will also need to stretch the waistline as you sew.

27 Once sewn, press the inner waistband downwards and pin in place, avoiding any puckering of the fabric. Stitch this in place 1cm (⅜in) away from the overlocked edge, leaving a 2.5cm (1in) gap to insert the elastic. This will create a hidden channel within the dress.

28 Cut your waist elastic strip following the pattern measurement. Attach a safety pin to one end and use this to feed it through the waistline channel. Bring both the short ends together and stitch together with a regular 1cm (⅜in) seam allowance before topstitching the gap in the waistline closed.

28

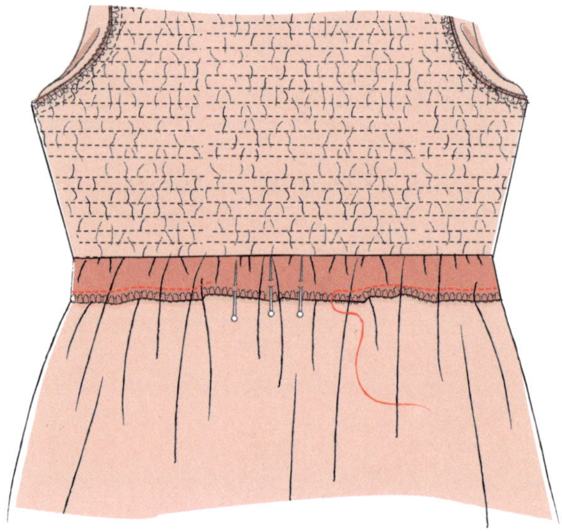

Finishing the dress

29 Fold each of the waist-tie pieces in half along the length and pin in place. Sew down the long edge and continue along one short edge. Clip the corners, turn out and press.

30 Baste both waist-tie pieces together along the remaining short edge. The raw edge will be hidden within the waistband and will act as a marker for the centre point.

31 Attach a safety pin to one end of the waist tie and gently feed it through both of the buttonhole openings. Make sure the centre point join falls in the centre of the buttonholes. Use a few small stitches to secure this in place from the outside of the waistband and tie a neat bow.

32 Try on your dress to check you're happy with the length and adjust as necessary.

33 Sew a narrow 0.2cm (⅛in) hem, as in step 6. Alternatively, you could use a rolled-hem foot on lighter-weight fabrics.

34 Remove any remaining gathering stitches that may be visible and give the dress a final press.

30

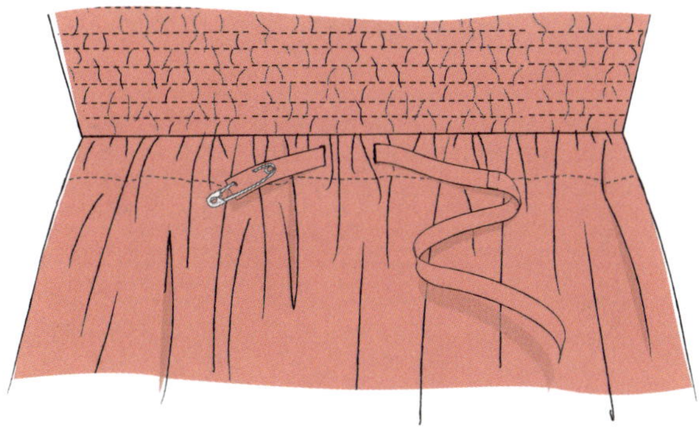

Woo!

I've said it before, and I'll say it again... shirring is the cutest technique ever! I just know your dress is going to fit you like a glove. I hope you feel amazing in it.

Styling suggestion

I can guarantee this will be one of the most versatile pieces in your wardrobe. For those sunny days, pop on your dress with some statement sandals and sunnies and you're good to go. For the colder months, pair your long-sleeved top with a knitted vest for a cute yet cosy combo!

VARIATION

Shirred top, long sleeve, ruffle peplum

It couldn't be easier to make this top variation – the shirring naturally produces a waist peplum without the need for any extra pattern pieces. This version is a quicker sew so opt for the top if you're short on time. The long sleeves have just the right amount of puff to add some interest while keeping it casual, but you could, of course, mix and match with the shorter sleeves depending on your preference.

Finished length measurements

	6	8	10	12	14	16	18	20	22
Front length (cm)	42.8	43.4	44	44.6	45.2	45.8	46.4	47	47.6
Front length (in)	16¾	17	17¼	17½	17¾	18	18¼	18½	18¾
Sleeve length (cm)	66.7	67.2	67.7	68.2	68.7	69.2	69.7	70.2	70.7
Sleeve length (in)	26¼	26½	26⅝	26¾	27	27¼	27½	27⅝	27¾

Fabric requirements

- All sizes: 1.5m (1¾yd) of main fabric, 150cm (60in) wide
- For additional notions required, see page 106

Making the variation

1 Cut out your pattern pieces, making sure to choose the correct size shirring panels for the top.

2 Follow the instructions for the dress, stopping after you've added the sleeves. As there is no skirt to add, you can simply try on your top to check you are happy with the length.

3 Sew a narrow hem as you did with the neckline frill, or you could use a rolled-hem foot on lighter-weight fabrics if you prefer.

Top tip!

If you'd like a bit more coverage, leave excess fabric at the bottom of the peplum and cut this down to your desired length after your final try-on.

Cutting guide

1 Long sleeve – cut 2

2 Bodice front – cut 1 on fold on shirred fabric

3 Bodice back – cut 1 on fold on shirred fabric

4 Collar frill – cut 1

5 Shirred panel – cut 2

All sizes: 150cm (60in) wide fabric

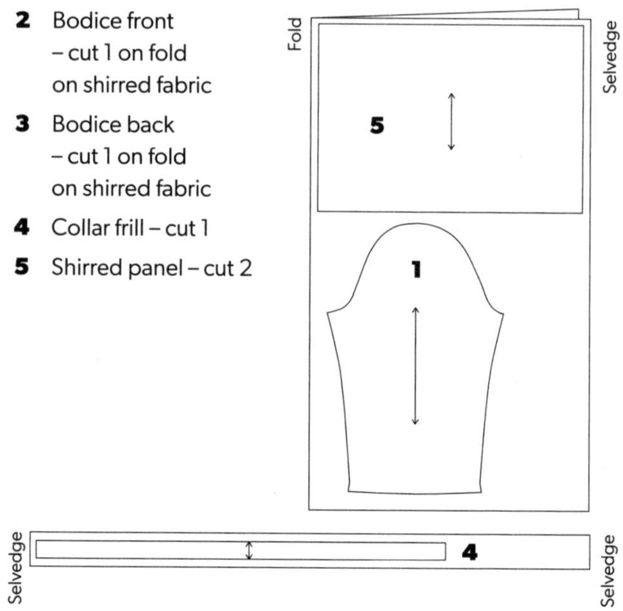

Technique Tutorial: *Shirring*

I feel like I have to start this tutorial with a disclaimer: shirring can be tricky to get the hang of as a beginner and different machines require different settings to get the perfect result. I'm going to share with you all my top tips for being successful at shirring, but please do bear in mind that you may have to play around with your own machine to find what works best for you. Have the patience to get this right – it's so worth it!

Preparing your project

Buy some shirring elastic: There can be a lot of different options on the market when it comes to elastic. I have always used cheaper elastic threads that can be found in most craft shops or local markets and have never had any issues. Try searching for shirring elastic on eBay and you will be able to find lots of options.

Thread up your machine: Your machine will need to be threaded up with regular sewing thread as usual. Make sure to pick a thread that perfectly matches the fabric you are using as it will be visible on the front of your garment.

Wind your bobbin: Rather than using regular thread on your bobbin, we will instead wind it with the shirring elastic. This will need to be done by hand. When winding it on, you should have a small amount of tension in the elastic to keep it neatly on the bobbin without overly stretching it.

Insert your bobbin: Place your bobbin into your machine as usual, making sure the elastic properly goes through the tension discs. Rather than letting the machine pull the elastic up to the top like usual, use your hand wheel to manually do this. When the upper thread catches the elastic, it will pull it up and through to the top.

Find the perfect settings: This is where it gets difficult to give specifics, as all machines like to shir slightly differently. You will need to increase your stitch length to its maximum and then find the tension that works best for you. I turn my machine tension right up to 9 but I know this doesn't work for other machines. Start with your tension at around a 5 and sew a swatch on some test fabric. If the tension is too loose, the elastic will look wiggly on the back of your fabric, and it won't gather in. If this happens, turn your tension up slightly and try again!

Re-wind: If your tension is still too loose, or your fabric is not gathering in, and you have tried all the different tension settings, the problem will probably lie with the way you have wound your bobbin. Try winding it again with more or less tension than before and repeat.

Shirring your fabric

1 Before sewing directly onto your fabric, you may want to draw lines to follow. Use the pattern markings as a guide and use a ruler with a reliable fabric pen (Pilot Frixion pens are my favourite) to draw on the lines. However, if you are confident sewing in a straight line following the markings on your machine stitch plate/presser foot, then feel free to skip this step.

2 Begin by sewing your first line of shirring. Make sure to sew a few reverse stitches at the beginning and end of each row to keep the elastic in place. As you sew, you should be stretching the fabric to make sure it lays flat. This will help you to keep your rows of stitching straight, too.

3 Don't be afraid if the first few rows look a little looser than you expect – the fabric will naturally tighten up as you sew more rows!

4 Shirring does use quite a lot of elastic, so you will likely have to stop to rewind your bobbin multiple times throughout. Try to keep the tension you are winding at the same as before.

5 Once you have finished all the rows of stitches, trim the excess threads and give the full piece of shirring a really good steam with an iron. This will shrink the stitches in further and help them to look even.

Woo!

Hopefully all these tips will help you to produce some neat shirring. It's one of those techniques that can be hard to master at first. But once you've found the settings that are best for your machine, it works every time. Don't be surprised if you end up with lots of shirred pieces in your wardrobe!

THE BIB DRESS

Vintage silhouette, A-line skirt, button detail

In my own handmade wardrobe, there are a lot of items with a vintage/retro vibe so, of course, I wanted to channel this timeless style in the book. The main feature of this design is the unique bib detail that takes it from a simple A-line dress to something extra special. Prepare yourself for lots of people asking where you got your outfit from when you're wearing this! As always, how bold you want to go with the dress is completely up to you. I absolutely love creating a contrast with the bib panel, but it looks equally pretty all in the same print to keep it more casual. You can also play around with adding a bow or even buttons to the centre to further customize your look.

Fabric suggestions

- Viscose/viscose sateen
- Duchess satin (this will give a more structured look to occasion-wear)
- Brocade/jacquard

Notions

- Sizes 6–14: 1.8m (2yd) of main fabric, 150cm (60in) wide
  Sizes 16–22: 2.3m (2½yd) of main fabric, 150cm (60in) wide
- 0.6m (¾yd) of lining fabric, 150cm (60in) wide
- Light-/medium-weight iron-on woven interfacing of a similar weight to your chosen fabric
- 56cm (22in) invisible zip
- Four 1cm (⅜in) buttons for cuffs (and extra for the bib, if desired)
- Optional: hook-and-eye fastening

Notes

- All seams should be sewn with a 1cm (⅜in) seam allowance unless otherwise stated.
- Read through the technique tutorial on gathering (page 64), invisible zips (page 142) and buttonholes (page 162) before you begin.
- Conversions to imperial measurements aren't always precise as they often need to be rounded up or down, but they do work with the patterns. Stick with either the metric or imperial measurements – don't mix and match.

Finished measurements

	6	8	10	12	14	16	18	20	22
Bust (cm)	86.6	91.6	96.6	101.6	106.6	111.6	116.6	121.6	126.6
Bust (in)	34	36	38	40	42	44	46	48	50
Waist (cm)	68.2	73.2	78.2	83.2	88.2	93.2	98.2	103.2	108.2
Waist (in)	26¾	28¾	30¾	32¾	34¾	36¾	38½	40½	42½
Top hip (cm) 10cm from waist	83	88	93	98	103	108	113	118	123
Top hip (in) 4in from waist	32½	34½	36½	38½	40½	42½	44½	46½	48½
Low hip (cm) 20cm from waist	93	98	103	108	113	118	123	128	133
Low hip (in) 8in from waist	36½	38½	40½	42½	44½	46½	48½	50½	52½
Front hem width (cm)	57.6	60.1	62.6	65.1	67.6	70.1	72.6	75.1	77.6
Front hem width (in)	22½	23½	24⅝	25½	26½	27½	28½	29½	30½
Front length (cm)	89.5	90.1	90.7	91.3	91.9	92.5	93.1	93.7	94.3
Front length (in)	35¼	35½	35¾	36	36¼	36½	36⅝	36¾	37
Sleeve length (cm)	56.3	56.8	57.3	57.8	58.3	58.8	59.3	59.8	60.3
Sleeve length (in)	22	22¼	22½	22¾	23	23⅛	23¼	23½	23¾

Cutting guide

1 Front bodice – cut 1 main and 1 lining on fold
2 Back bodice – cut 2 main and 2 lining
3 Skirt front – cut 1 on fold
4 Skirt back – cut 2
5 Bib – cut 1 main and 1 lining on fold
6 Bib frill – cut 1
7 Cuff – cut 4 main and 2 interfacing
8 Sleeve placket – cut 2 main and 2 interfacing
9 Sleeve placket binding – cut 2 main and 2 interfacing
10 Cuff frill – cut 2
11 Sleeve – cut 2

All sizes: 150cm (60in) wide main fabric

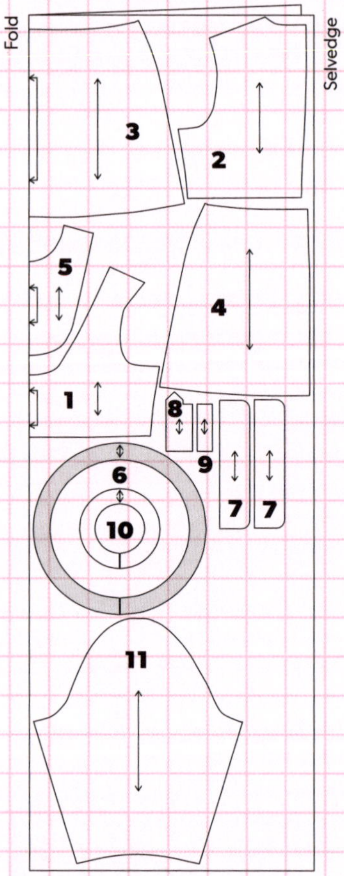

All sizes: 150cm (60in) wide lining fabric

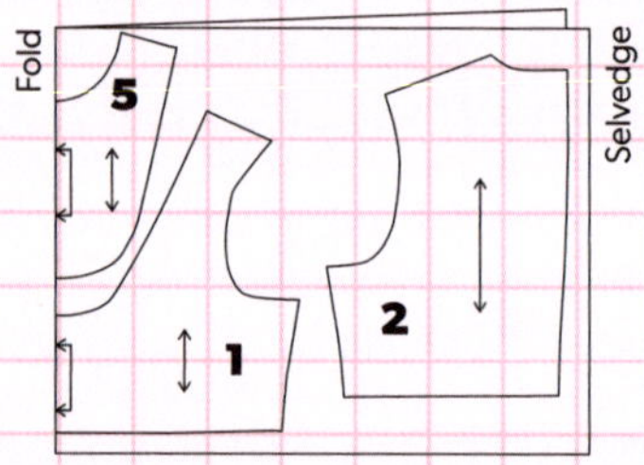

Interfacing

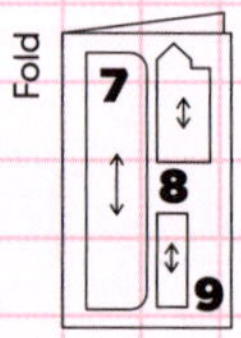

Pattern prep

1 Cut out the fabric pieces and transfer markings, including the darts. Iron fusible interfacing onto two of the cuff pieces and the cuff plackets.

2 Sew the darts on the front and back bodice pieces for both the main fabric and the lining and press towards the side seams.

3 Prepare the bib frill by finishing the outside edge with a narrow double turned hem. To do this, sew a line of stitching 0.2cm (⅛in) away from the frill edge. Use this as a guide to press under the 0.2cm (⅛in) to the wrong side of the fabric and stitch in place. Press under 0.2cm (⅛in) again and topstitch to enclose all the raw edges.

4 Run two rows of gathering stitches along the other long edge of the frill (see my technique tutorial on gathering on page 64).

5 Start by pinning the centre point of the ruffle to the centre front of the bib with right sides together. Gently pull on the gathering stitches and gather the ruffle to be the same length as the outer bib edge. Baste in place.

5

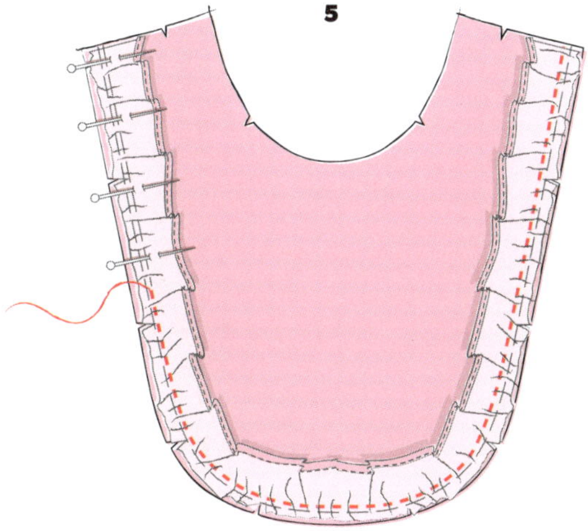

Completing the bodice

6 Place the bib right sides together with the bodice front, matching the centre fronts. Continue pinning all the way round the curve, matching notches as you go. Stitch in place then clip into the curve before pressing the seam allowance and frill downwards.

7 Repeat step 6 to join the bib lining and front bodice lining together.

8 Place the completed bodice front right sides together with the bodice back and pin together at the shoulder and side seams. The raw edge of the frill should be sandwiched between the shoulder seam also. Stitch in place and press the seam allowances towards the back. Repeat for the front and back bodice lining.

8

9 Place your bodice lining right sides together with the main bodice and pin together along the neckline edge. Stitch this seam with a regular 1cm (⅜in) seam allowance. Carefully clip into the seam allowance around the curve (this will help the neckline to lie flat) before pressing the bodice lining towards the wrong side of the bodice. We will now treat the main bodice and bodice lining as one.

Attaching the skirt & zip

13

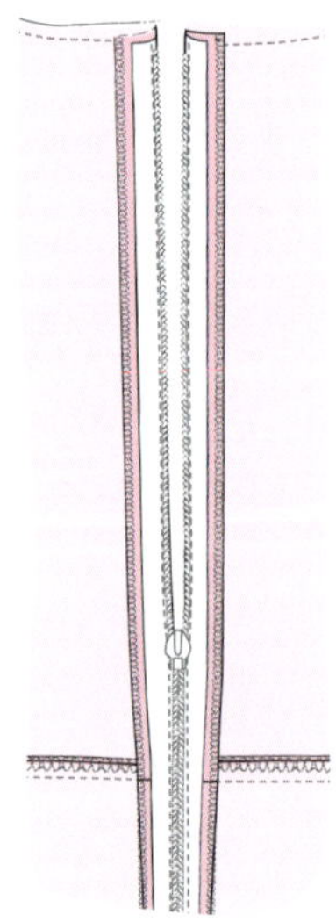

10 Place the skirt front and back pieces right sides together and pin at the side seams, matching notches. Stitch in place. Overlock (or zigzag) the raw edges and press the seam allowances towards the back.

11 Pin the completed skirt to the main bodice along the waistline, ensuring the side seams match perfectly and that the bodice lining is also caught in. Stitch in place and press the seam allowance upwards.

12 Finish the raw edges along each side of the centre back on the overlocker (or zigzag). This should run all the way from the neckline edge of the bodice to the hem edge of the skirt, ensuring that the bodice lining is lying completely flat against the main bodice and that the raw edges line up.

13 Insert the invisible zip in the centre-back seam. The raw edge of the zipper tape should align with the raw edge of the neckline, and it should finish in line with the zipper notch. (See page 142 for how to insert the perfect invisible zip.)

14 Once happy with the placement, sew up the remainder of the centre-back seam and press the seam open.

Making the sleeves

15 First, prepare the cuff frill in the same way as you did for the bib frill with a narrow hem on one long edge and gathering stitches on the other.

16 Take one main sleeve piece and carefully cut along the placket placement line. At the end of the line, snip a Y-shape, cutting no further than 1cm (⅜in) into the fabric. This Y-shaped cut will give more room to turn the placket to the right side of the fabric later.

17 With right sides together, fold the sleeve in half to bring the underarm edges together and sew the seam. Finish the raw edge on the overlocker (or zigzag) and press the seam towards the back of the sleeve.

18 Taking the cuff frill, gently pull on the gathering stitches until it is the same length as the lower edge of the main sleeve. Pin in place, making sure the raw edges of the frill line up with the raw edges of the placket cut line. The wrong side of the frill should be against the right side of the sleeve. Baste in place just inside the seam line.

19 Take the small sleeve-placket binding piece. Press it in half along the length, open it out and then press each long edge in to meet the central crease before folding the full piece in half again. Give it one final press while folded.

16

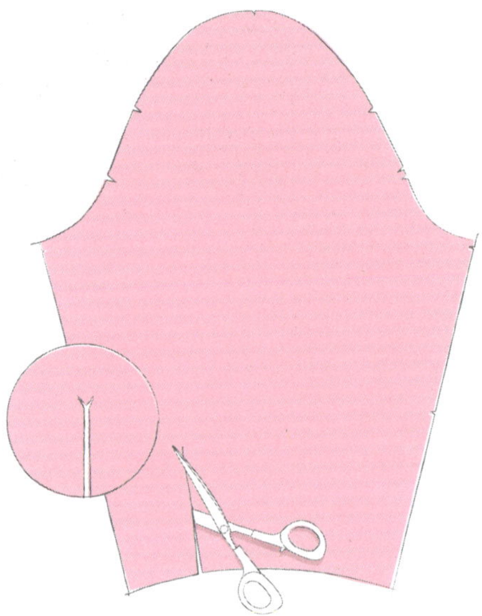

18

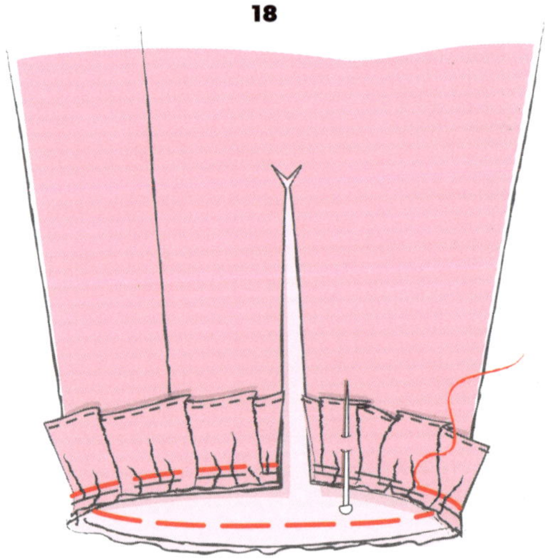

20 Take this binding piece and sandwich it around the raw edge of the placket opening closest to the sleeve back. Carefully edgestitch it in place along the long edge.

21 Place the right side of the sleeve-placket facing against the wrong side of the sleeve. Align the side furthest from the pointed tip with the remaining raw edge of the cut placket opening. Stitch in place.

22 Press the seam allowance towards the placket facing. Then press under 1cm (⅜in) along the remaining long edge of the placket facing and along each side of the pointed tip. This will encase all the raw edges.

23 Fold the placket over towards the right side of the sleeve along the marked fold line and pin to the front of the sleeve. Topstitch in place along the long edge.

24 Make sure the binding is correctly in line beneath the placket. Topstitch along the short ends of the long pointed edge before pivoting and stitching back across. You should catch in the binding on the underside when doing this topstitching. Make sure to consult the illustration to see what your stitch line should look like. Repeat for the second sleeve.

25 We will now finish the cuff. Take your interfaced cuff piece and press under 1cm (⅜in) along the upper edge. Place both cuffs (one interfaced, one not) right sides together and pin around the outer curved edge, keeping the 1cm (⅜in) pressed under. Stitch in place. Clip the curves and turn right sides out.

20

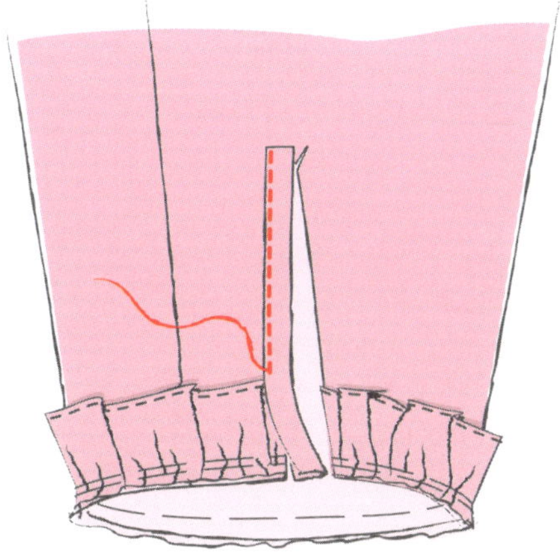

21

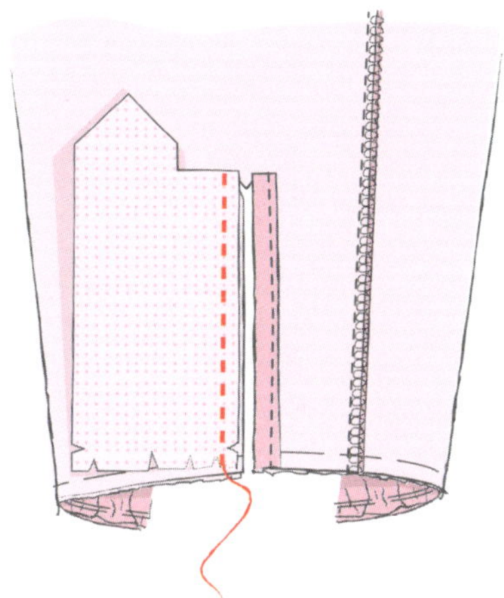

24

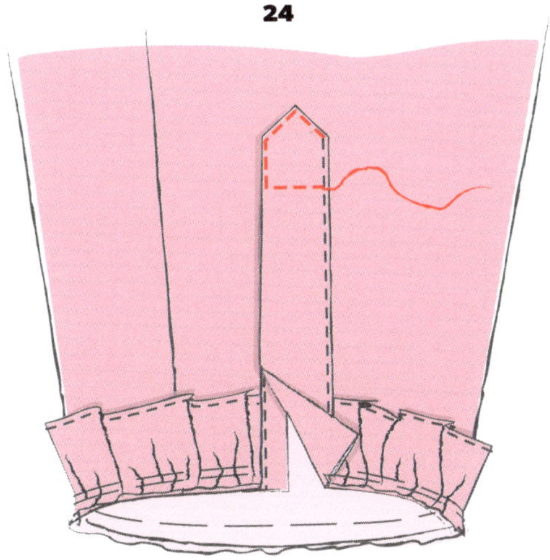

26 Pin the uninterfaced side of the cuff to the bottom edge of the sleeve, making sure that the pressed-under edge is not caught up. Stitch in place. Press the seam allowance down towards the cuff.

27 To finish the inside of the cuff, topstitch from the right side of the cuff or hand stitch in place with invisible stitches, depending on your preference. Repeat for both sleeves.

28 Sew the two buttonholes on both cuffs at the pattern markings (see page 162 for my technique tutorial on buttonholes if needed). Cut out the centre and trim any excess threads.

29 Along each sleeve head, run two rows of gathering stitches between the notches.

30 Pin the sleeves to the bodice armholes, first matching the underarm seams and notches. Gently pull on the gathering stitches to gather the sleeve into the sleeve head. Pin well before stitching in place. Overlock the raw edges and press the seam allowances up into the sleeve.

26

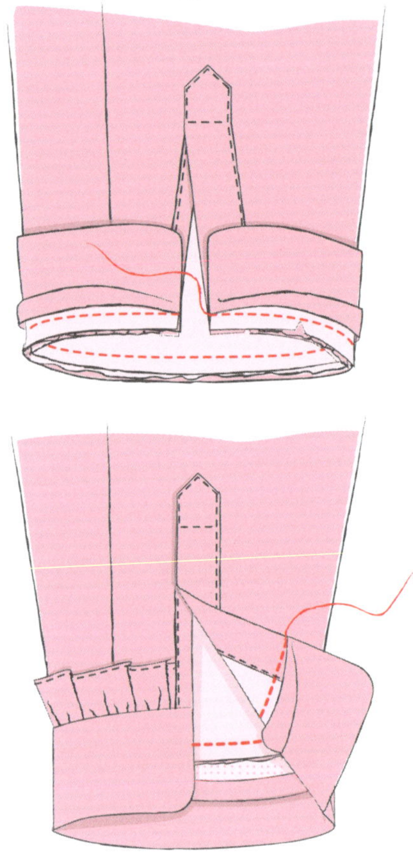

Finishing touches

31 Hand sew two buttons to each cuff to correspond with the buttonholes and add buttons to the bib as well if you'd like.

32 Try on your dress to check you're happy with the length and make any adjustments necessary.

33 Once happy, finish the dress hem with a narrow double-turned hem, as on the bodice frill.

34 If needed, hand sew a hook and eye to the top of your zip to help it sit perfectly closed at the neckline.

Woo!

Wow, those sleeves were a challenge, but you did it! If you want my advice, go book an afternoon tea for yourself and a friend so you can give your new garment the outing she deserves!

VARIATION

Peplum top, bow detail

I absolutely love the bib dress but wow, doesn't it also look great as a top? This variation features a cute bow for some extra sass, which you could feature as a contrast or sew in the same fabric as the top depending on your preference. The top uses the same cuffed sleeves that complete the vintage-inspired look.

Finished length measurements

	6	8	10	12	14	16	18	20	22
Front length (cm)	59	59.6	60.2	60.8	61.4	62	62.6	63.2	63.8
Front length (in)	23¼	23½	23¾	24	24⅛	24½	24⅝	24¾	25

Cutting guide

1 Front bodice – cut 1 main and 1 lining on fold

2 Back bodice – cut 2 main and 2 lining

3 Top peplum – cut 1

4 Bib – cut 1 main and 1 lining on fold

5 Bib frill – cut 1

6 Cuff – cut 4 main and 2 interfacing

7 Sleeve placket – cut 2 main and 2 interfacing

8 Sleeve placket binding – cut 2 main and 2 interfacing

9 Cuff frill – cut 2

10 Sleeve – cut 2

11 Bow – cut 1 main and 1 interfacing on fold

12 Bow centre – cut 1 on fold

Note: fabric requirements are listed on page 141.

All sizes: 150cm (60in) wide fabric

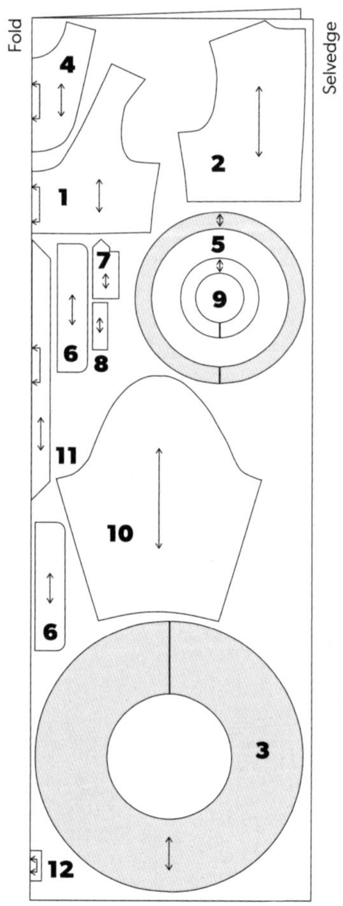

All sizes: 150cm (60in) lining fabric

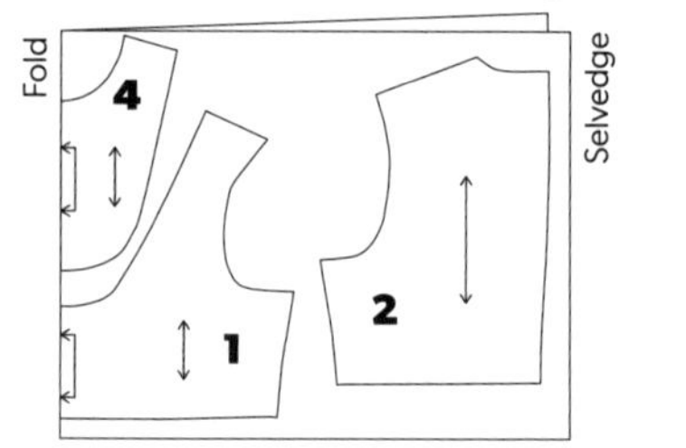

Interfacing

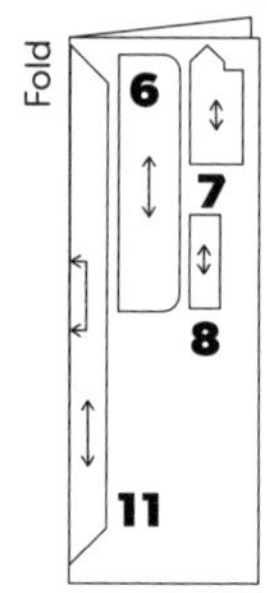

Fabric requirements

- All sizes: 2.25m (2½yd) of main fabric, 150cm (60in) wide
- For additional notions required, see page 126

Making the variation

1 Cut out your pattern pieces using the cutting layout for the top variation and follow the instructions for making the bodice of the dress.

2 Take the bow piece and fold it in half, right sides together. Sew it up, leaving a 2.5cm (1in) gap in the centre of the long edge. Use the gap to turn out the bow to the right side. Press the bow well and edgestitch (stitch close to the edge of the seam). This will close up the gap in the seam allowance and create a smart finish.

3 Manipulate the strip into a flat bow shape as per the illustration. Play around with it until the bow looks to be giving you the desired shape and baste it together in the centre. This will be covered by the centre of the bow, so it doesn't need to be neat.

4 Prepare the bow centre by folding the strip in half to match the long edges. Sew along the long edge and one end, leaving the opposite end open to turn the strip out. Turn out and press well.

5 Wrap the bow centre around the middle of the main bow. You should be able to bring the ends together and stitch to hold in place. Manoeuvre the bow centre piece so that the seam is hidden at the back of the bow.

3

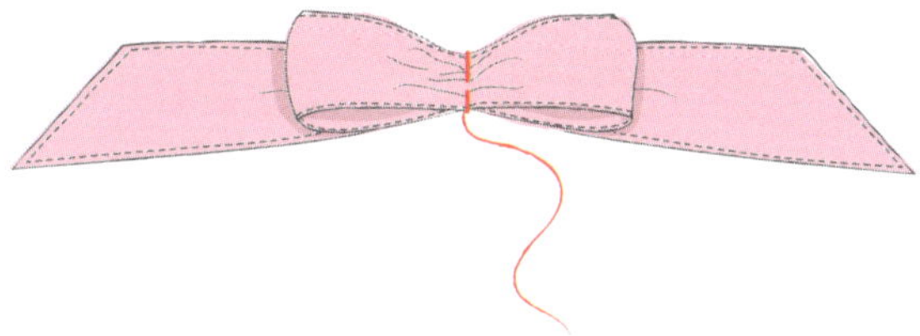

6

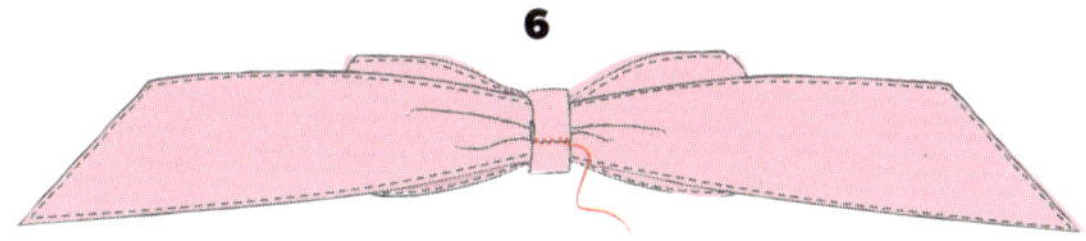

6 Following the marking on the pattern piece, hand sew the bow to the centre front of the bib. Start by stitching on the bow centre then attach the rest of the bow at multiple points to ensure it is supported enough on the top.

7 Pin the peplum to the bodice and attach it in the same way as the dress skirt – it's essentially just a shorter version!

8 As with the dress, give your top a quick try-on before hemming the peplum with a narrow hem. You may want to add a hook and eye to the top of the zip depending on your preference. You can simply hand sew this on if desired.

Styling suggestion

If ultra-feminine isn't your vibe, try pairing your bib top with a leather skirt or trousers to add a bit of an edge. It's the perfect date-night outfit!

Technique Tutorial: *Invisible zips*

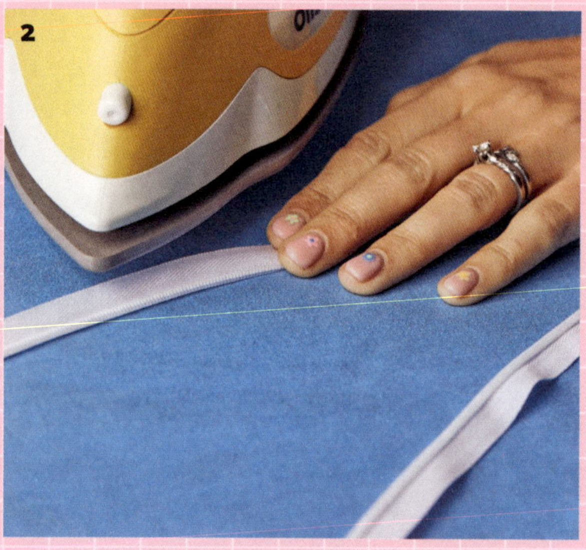

An invisible zip makes a garment look super chic, and mastering the process of inserting one is a key technique for any keen sewer. It's not inserted in the same way as a standard zip, so read on. Over my many years of sewing, I have learned that preparation is key for a neat finish. You might be tempted to rush ahead and insert your zip in one go, but slowing down and taking time to perfect it will give you a much better finish overall. Let's do it!

1 First, finish the raw edges of the seam you are going to be working with using an overlocker or zigzag stitch.

2 Open your zip as far as it will go and, using a very low heat on your iron, gently press the teeth away from the zip. This will allow you to get as close to the zip as possible when sewing, which helps it to be fully invisible. Be careful not to use too high a heat as you risk melting the zip teeth!

3 With right sides together, pin the right-hand side of the zip to the left-hand side of the seam. Baste this in place using a long basting stitch (this will be removed once the zip is fully inserted).

4 You can either use your regular machine foot or switch to an invisible-zipper foot. If using a regular foot, some machines require you to move your needle position over to the left-hand side to allow you to get as close as possible to the zip teeth. Returning to a regular stitch length, sew the zip in place.

Top tip! If you love the look of invisible/concealed zips, an invisible-zipper foot is a good investment. These have grooves underneath that the zip teeth slide into, and this helps you sew really close to those teeth without accidentally sewing on them.

5 Find a recognizable point along your zip that you will be able to match with the opposite side – this is usually the waistline seam. Cut a small notch into the side of the zip where we have just sewn at that point. Close the zip and transfer the same notch to the other side of the zip that we are about to sew. This will help make sure the waistline matches up on both sides.

6 Now repeat the basting process for the opposite side of the zip, making sure that the notch matches with the waistline seam. Once basted, close the zip to check everything is lining up. If changes need to be made, you can unpick the basting and try again. If not, go ahead and stitch the zip in place.

7 Close the zip and admire your work! Gently press the fabric away from the zip, avoiding the zip teeth. You can also go in and unpick any visible basting stitches.

8 The final step is to close the remainder of the seam. Flip your skirt pieces so that right sides are together as usual and pin in place. Starting from the hem edge of the garment, sew the seam closed and continue as close as possible to where the zip finishes. This can be quite tricky due to the bulkiness at the base of the zip, so you may want to finish the very bottom with a couple of hand stitches if you struggle to get your machine stitches close enough.

Woo! And voila! You can now breathe a sigh of relief because the zip is complete. I would say that this is one of those techniques that just gets easier with practice, so don't be afraid to buy a few extra zips and have a go at inserting them into some scrap fabric if you are struggling. They can easily be unpicked and reused for your final project.

THE SHIRT DRESS

Mini-length, ruffle collar & shoulder detail

On those day when I'm struggling to decide what to wear, 99% of the time I'll be reaching for a shirt dress! They are such versatile pieces, and often come with a lot of ease at the waistline so they're cool and comfortable to wear. With me being me, of course I had to add a little extra sparkle to an otherwise standard shirt dress, so I decided to include the dreamiest double frill across the shoulders. If that feels too much for you, feel free to add only one layer, or leave it off completely – as always, these patterns are made to be played around with to suit your own style.

Fabric suggestions

For an extra-special make, look out for fabrics that include an embroidered border edge. You can cut the sleeve or hemline along this border to make it a unique feature on your dress! Try:

- Viscose
- Linen and linen blends
- Chambray or lightweight denim

Notions

- Sizes 6–14: 2.75m (3yd) of main fabric, 150cm (60in) wide. Sizes 16–22: 3m (3¼yd) of main fabric, 150cm (60in) wide
- Buttonhole foot
- 1cm (⅜in) buttons: seven for the ruffle collar, or eight for the grandad-collar version
- Iron-on woven interfacing of a similar weight to your chosen fabric

Notes

- All seams should be sewn together with a 1cm (⅜in) seam allowance unless otherwise stated.
- Read through the technique tutorials on gathering (page 64), bias binding (page 100) and buttonholes (page 162) before you begin.
- Conversions to imperial measurements aren't always precise as they often need to be rounded up or down, but they do work with the patterns. Stick with either the metric or imperial measurements – don't mix and match.

Finished measurements

	6	8	10	12	14	16	18	20	22
Bust (cm)	93	98	103	108	113	118	123	128	133
Bust (in)	36½	38½	40½	42½	44½	46½	48½	50½	52½
Waist (cm)	92	97	102	107	112	117	122	127	132
Waist (in)	36¼	38	40	42	44	46	48	50	52
Top hip (cm) 10cm from waist	102	107	112	117	122	127	132	137	142
Top hip (in) 4in from waist	40	42	44	46	48	50	52	54	56
Low hip (cm) 20cm from waist	110.6	115.6	120.6	125.6	130.6	135.6	140.6	145.6	150.6
Low hip (in) 8in from waist	43½	45½	47½	49½	51½	53½	55⅜	57⅜	59¼
Front hem width (cm)	65.3	67.8	70.3	72.8	75.3	77.8	80.3	82.8	85.3
Front hem width (in)	25¾	26¾	27½	28½	29½	30½	31½	32½	33½
Front length (cm)	88.5	89.1	89.7	90.3	90.9	91.5	92.1	92.7	93.3
Front length (in)	34¾	35	35¼	35½	35¾	36	36¼	36½	36¾
Sleeve length (cm)	46.4	46.9	47.4	47.9	48.4	48.9	49.4	49.9	50.4
Sleeve length (in)	18¼	18½	18⅝	18¾	19	19¼	19⅜	19½	19¾

Cutting guide

1 Bodice front – cut 2

2 Bodice back – cut 1 on fold

3 Skirt front – cut 1 on fold

4 Skirt back – cut 1 on fold

5 Sleeve – cut 2

6 Keyhole binding – cut 2 on the bias (see page 82)

7 Sleeve tie binding – cut 2 on the bias (see page 82)

8 Neckline binding – cut 1 on the bias (see page 82)

9 Button placket – cut 2 main and 2 interfacing

10 Ruffle collar – cut 1 on fold

11 Upper ruffle – cut 1 on fold

12 Lower ruffle – cut 1 on fold

All sizes: 150cm (60in) wide fabric

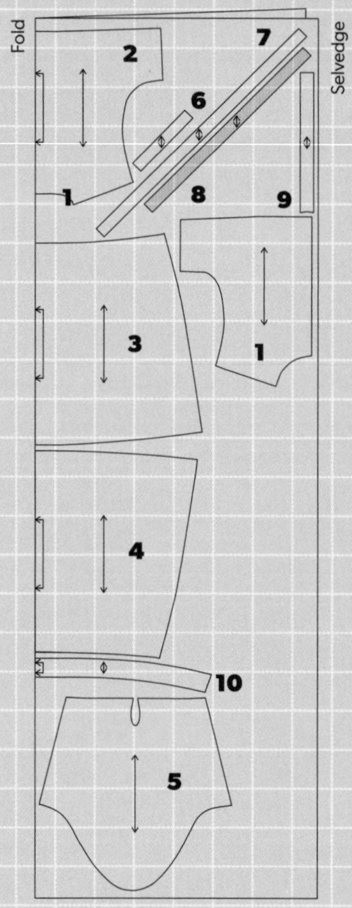

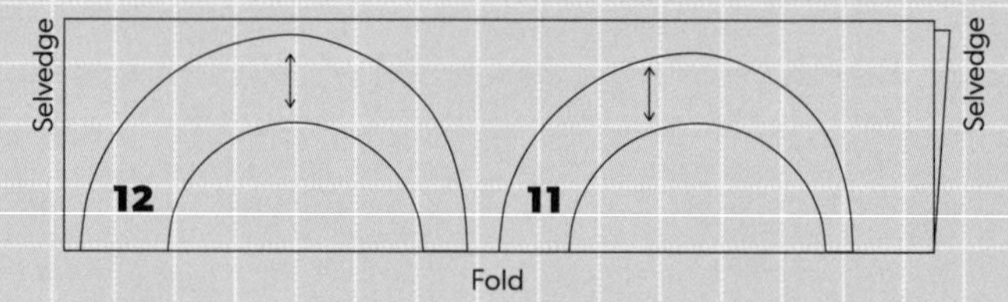

Interfacing

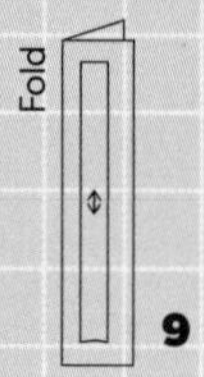

Pattern prep

1 Cut out the fabric pieces and transfer all notches and markings, taking particular care to mark the placement of the shoulder ruffle/frill, if you're including it. My favourite way to do this is with a Pilot Frixion pen, as you can draw directly on the fabric and remove it with the heat from your iron once the ruffle is attached. If you want to make use of a border design in your fabric, as I did, take your time positioning your pattern pieces so you can do so.

2 Apply iron-on interfacing to the wrong side of both button plackets.

Starting on the bodice

3 Place the bodice front pieces on top of the bodice back with right sides together. Pin along the shoulder seams and stitch in place. Finish the raw edges and press the seam allowances towards the back.

4 Sew a line of stay stitching along the neckline edge on the seam line (see pages 19 and 83).

Attaching the shoulder ruffle

5 First, finish the outer edge of the ruffles with a narrow double hem. To do this, sew a line of stitching 0.2cm (⅛in) away from the long outer edge. Use this as a guide to press under the 0.2cm (⅛in) to the wrong side of the fabric and stitch in place. Press under 0.2cm (⅛in) again and topstitch to enclose all the raw edges. This can be tricky as the edge is curved, so take your time.

6 Place the upper ruffle on top of the lower one with both right sides facing upwards. Pin them together along the inner raw edge and overlock (or zigzag) them together. We will now treat this as a single ruffle piece.

7 Run two rows of gathering stitches along the overlocked inner edge of the ruffle (see my technique tutorial on gathering on page 64).

8 Starting at the centre back of the bodice, place the ruffle right-side down on top. Align the overlocked edge with the markings we transferred and pin in place. Gently pull on the gathering stitches to gather the ruffle in until it fits along the marked line. Even out the gathers and pin in place, ensuring the short, raw edges are in line with the front edge of the bodice (these will eventually be enclosed in the button placket).

9 Stitch the ruffle in place, 1cm (⅜in) from the overlocked edge.

10 Turn the ruffle the correct way around and press it and the seam allowance downwards.

8

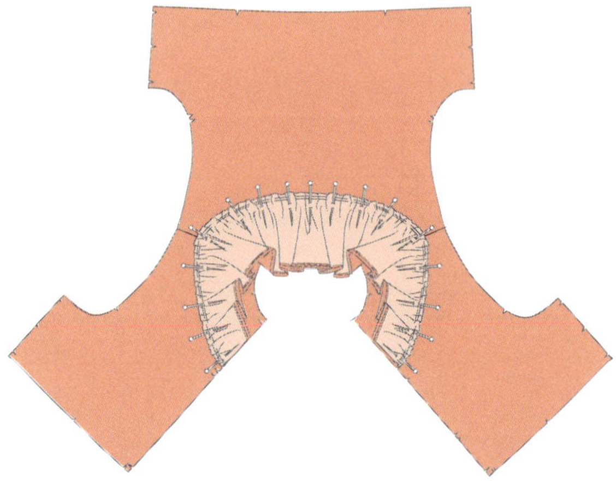

Constructing the bodice

11 Pin the bodice pieces right sides together at the side seams and stitch in place. Finish the raw edges on the overlocker (or zigzag) and press towards the back. Pin an interfaced placket piece right sides together to each of the front edges, matching notches, and sew with a 1cm (⅜in) seam allowance. Press the seam allowances towards the placket.

12 Press under 1cm (⅜in) along the remaining long edge of the button placket before pressing the full placket in half. The pressed-under edge should just cover the stitching line on the inside of the bodice.

13 With the correct side of the bodice and placket facing upwards, stitch in the ditch to keep the placket in place (this means stitching right on the seam).

13

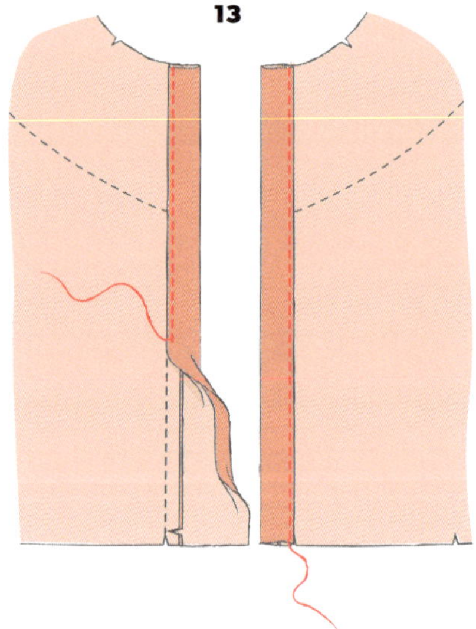

Top tip!

Depending on the look you are going for, you may wish to topstitch down each of the long edges of the placket to give an even cleaner finish.

14 Using the buttonhole markings transferred from the pattern piece, sew seven buttonholes along the left placket. Make sure to use my handy technique tutorial on buttonholes (see page 162).

15 Once the buttonholes are complete, hand stitch the buttons on the right placket, making sure they directly line up with the holes.

16 Do up all seven buttons in the correct buttonholes. Align the bottom raw edge of the placket and baste in place.

17

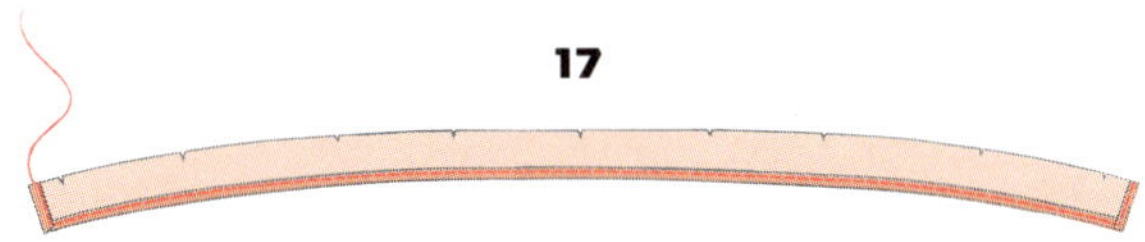

18

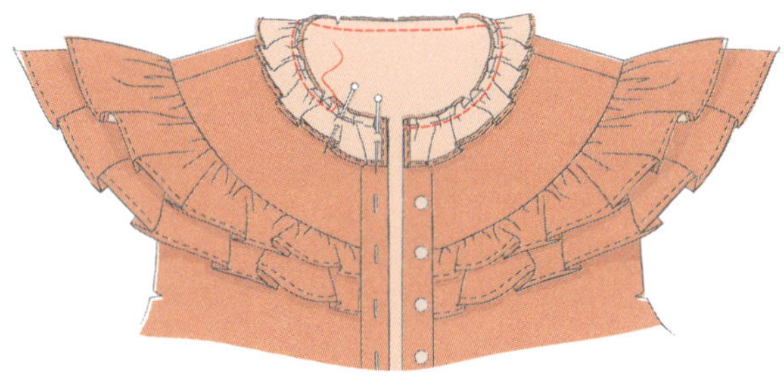

20

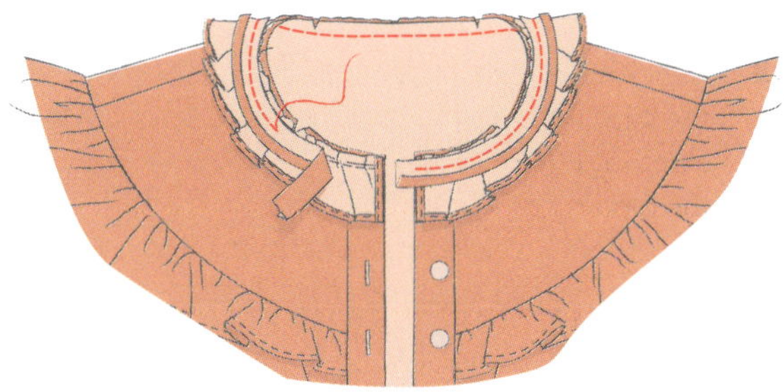

Attaching the ruffle collar

17 Finish the upper edge of the ruffle collar with a narrow double hem as you did for the shoulder ruffles. Repeat to hem each of the short ends.

18 Run two rows of gathering stitches along the remaining long edge of the ruffle collar piece. Gently pull on the gathering stitches and gather to be the same length as the neckline edge. Pin in place, starting from the centre back. Make sure that the front edge of the collar and placket are completely in line. Stitch in place.

19 Take your neckline bias-binding strip. Press it in half with wrong sides together, open it out then press each of the long raw edges in to meet the central crease before pressing in half again. This will create a very narrow binding to finish the raw edge at the neckline. Alternatively, you may wish to use a piece of narrow ready-made binding.

20 Open out one long edge of the binding and align the crease with the stitch line of the neck edge. Stitch on top of the previous line of stitching and down the centre of the binding crease, making sure to leave an overhang of about 1.5cm (⅝in) of binding on each end of the neckline.

21 Trim the raw edge of the neckline down so it is in line with the raw edge of the binding.

22 Fold the excess short ends of the binding inwards to encase the raw edge, then fold the binding in half before pinning to the neckline. No raw edges should be visible, and make sure that the collar is up and out of the way before you sew. Topstitch the binding in place at just under 1cm (3⁄8in), taking care not to create any puckers in your fabric.

23 Press the ruffle collar upwards.

Adding the sleeves

24 For each sleeve you have a short binding strip for the keyhole opening, and one longer piece for the ties. Press the strips as in step 19 for the ruffle collar.

25 To finish the keyhole opening, open out one edge of the binding and pin to the opening edge with right sides together. Stitch down following the crease in the binding.

26 Press the binding to the wrong side of the fabric and pin in place just past the original stitch line to enclose all the raw edges. Topstitch in place from the right side of the fabric. Trim the excess binding from the cuff edge of the sleeve.

27 Fold the keyhole in half so that the binding evenly overlaps. At the top centre point, sew a very small diagonal line through the binding.

28 Now, with right sides together, sew the sleeve underarm seam. Finish the raw edges and press towards the back.

29 Press under 1cm (3⁄8in) at each end of the remaining binding strip to enclose the raw edge. Open out the long edge of the binding and match the centre points of the binding and sleeve. Pin in place, with right sides together, then stitch following the binding crease, beginning at one sleeve edge and finishing at the other.

25

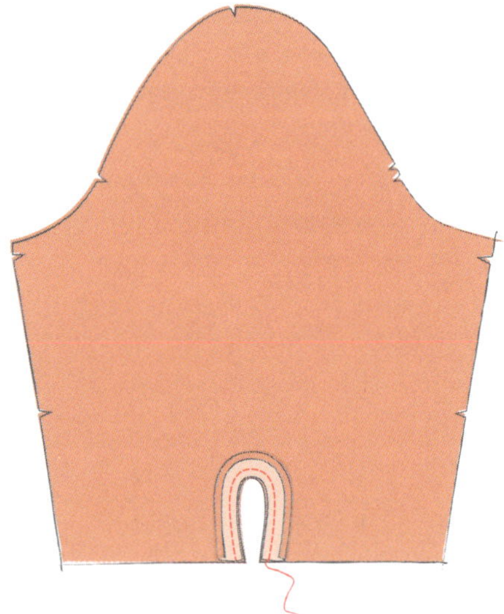

27

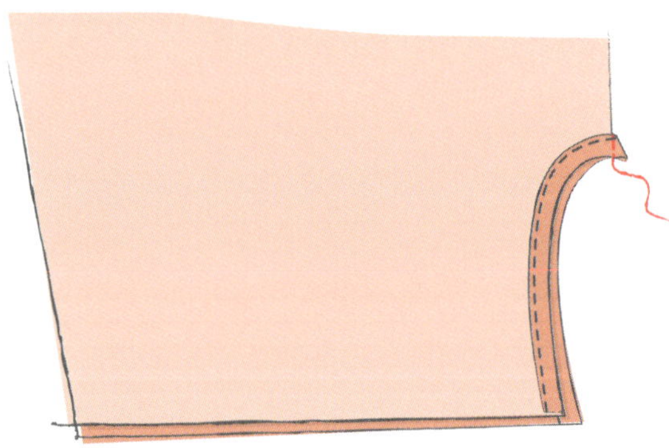

30 Now fold the binding round to the other side of the sleeve edge, so it just covers the line of stitching. Edgestitch all the way from one end of the sleeve tie to the other. You will need to make sure the binding is folded evenly in half in order to catch the binding in on the inside of the sleeve and ensure the sleeve ties look even. This can be quite fiddly to do, so take your time.

31 Finally, it's time to set in the sleeves! With right sides together, pin the sleeve into the armhole, first matching the underarm seams and notches, before evenly distributing the ease within the sleeve head. Stitch in place, finish the raw edges on the overlocker (or use zigzag) and press the seam allowance up into the sleeve head. Repeat for the second sleeve.

30

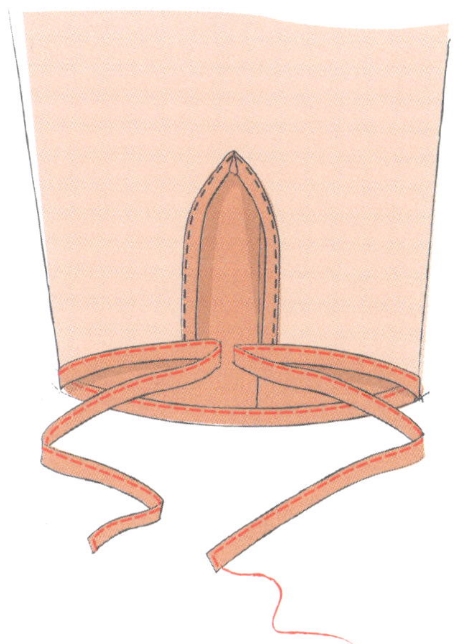

Attaching the skirt

32 With right sides together, pin the skirt front and back at the side seams and stitch in place. Finish the raw edges on the overlocker (or zigzag) and press towards the skirt back.

33 Pin the skirt to the waistline edge of the bodice with right sides together and sew. Finish the raw edges and press the seam allowance up towards the bodice.

Finishing touches

34 As always, it's a good idea to try on your dress and check you're happy with the length. Make any adjustments necessary.

35 To hem the dress, press under 1cm (⅜in) and then another 1.5cm (⅝in) along the hem edge before stitching in place.

36 Give everything a final press and remove any visible gathering stitches from the bodice ruffles.

Woo!

Now it's time for a pat on the back and an obligatory twirl in your new me-made dress. Nobody would ever guess just how much time and effort went into a simple shirt dress, but I promise you this will quickly become one of the most reached-for pieces in your wardrobe!

Styling suggestion

Nothing beats a cool linen dress in the summer. Try pairing your lovely new shirt dress with a pair of chunky sandals and a matching cross-body bag for the ultimate warm-weather look.

VARIATION

Midi- or maxi-length, grandad collar, simple silhouette

We all know how much I love frills and flourishes, but for those days when you feel like keeping your outfit more understated, I've designed a simpler variation. This dress features a grandad collar that gives it more of a classic shirt vibe, plus I've left off the shoulder frills. However, it wouldn't be Brogan style to leave it totally plain, so there's an optional ruffle skirt tier to take it from midi to maxi if the occasion allows it.

Finished measurements

	6	8	10	12	14	16	18	20	22
Front hem width (cm)	79.8	82.3	84.8	87.3	89.8	92.3	94.8	97.3	99.8
Front hem width (in)	31½	32½	33⅜	34⅜	35¼	36¼	37¼	38¼	39¼
Front length (cm)	136.2	136.8	137.4	138	138.6	139.2	139.8	140.4	141
Front length (in)	53½	53¾	54	54¼	54½	54¾	55	55¼	55½

Cutting guide

1 Bodice front – cut 2
2 Bodice back – cut 1 on fold
3 Skirt front – cut 1 on fold
4 Skirt back – cut 1 on fold
5 Sleeve – cut 2
6 Keyhole binding – cut 2
7 Sleeve tie binding – cut 2
8 Grandad collar – cut 2 main and 1 interfacing
9 Skirt ruffle front – cut 1 on fold
10 Skirt ruffle back – cut 1 on fold
11 Button placket – cut 2 main and 2 interfacing

Note: fabric requirements are listed on page 161.

All sizes: 150cm (60in) wide fabric

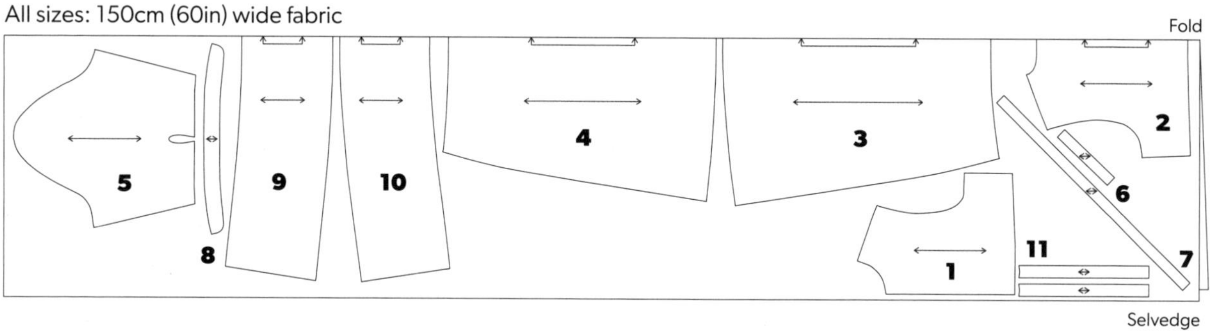

Fabric requirements

- All sizes: 3.5m (4yd) of main fabric, 150cm (60in) wide
- For additional notions required, see page 146

Making the variation

1 Cut out the fabric pieces using the alternative pattern for the long variation and transfer all notches and markings. Apply iron-on interfacing to the wrong side of both button plackets and one of the grandad collar pieces.

2 Start the bodice as instructed on page 149, then skip the instructions for the shoulder ruffle and carry on constructing the bodice.

3 There's no ruffle collar. Instead, press under 1cm (⅜in) along the bottom edge of the uninterfaced grandad collar piece.

4 With right sides together, pin the two collar pieces together, making sure that the 1cm (⅜in) is still pressed under. Sew around the outside edge but leave the bottom edge open.

5 Clip the curves around the collar and turn it right side out. Press well.

6 Pin the uninterfaced side of the collar to the neckline edge of the bodice, starting from the centre back and working your way round to the front edge. The edge of the collar and bodice should line up exactly. Sew in place, taking care not to catch in the interfaced collar as you do so.

7 Press the seam allowance upwards and pin in place, sandwiching it between the two sides of the collar. The pressed collar edge should just cover the previous stitching line. Topstitch in place, taking care to avoid any puckers in the fabric.

6

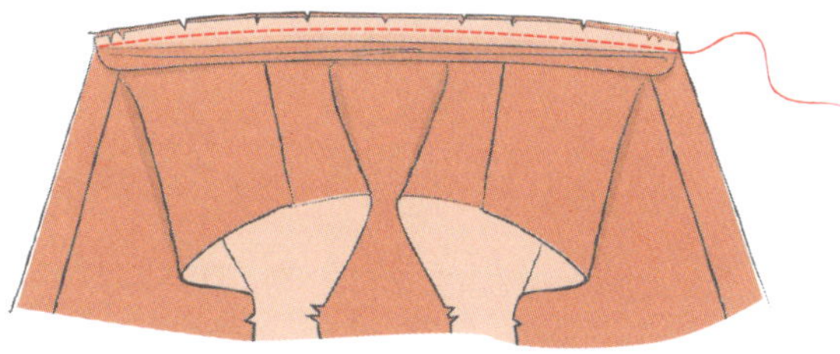

8 Add an extra buttonhole at the top of the collar and finish as you did on the bodice front.

9 Continue to follow the instructions for the Shirt Dress from step 24 onwards, attaching the sleeves and skirt. Once the main skirt is attached, you can add the optional bottom tier. First, sew the bottom tier together at the side seams as we did with the main skirt. Sew two rows of gathering stitches along the upper edge (see page 64).

10 Gently pull on the gathering stitches until the bottom tier is the same width as the upper skirt. Pin at the side seams and notches, before evenly distributing the gathers across the skirt. Stitch in place. Finish the raw edges and press the seam allowances upwards.

11 Finally, try on the dress to check the fit before hemming.

Technique Tutorial: *Buttonholes*

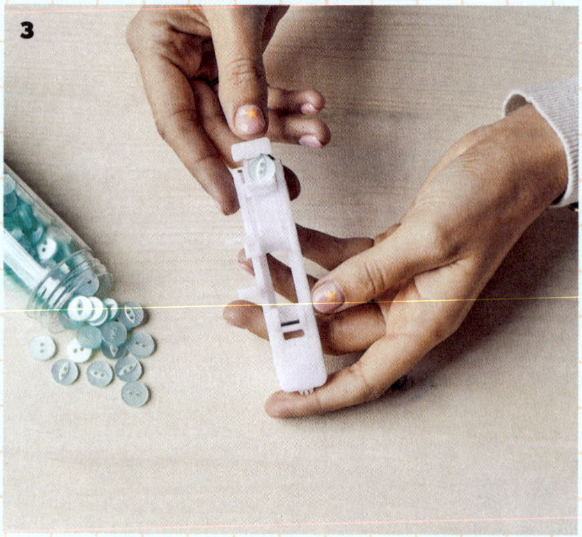

Buttonholes can often seem scary to less-experienced sewers but it's something that just gets easier with practice. Follow my top tips below to make the perfect buttonholes.

1 Transfer the buttonhole-placement markings from the pattern piece to your fabric. You can do this by simply putting a pin in the fabric or using a removable fabric pen such as a Pilot Frixion pen.

2 Measure the distance between your buttonholes to check they are even and make any changes necessary to even them up.

3 Moving over to your machine, swap out your regular presser foot for a buttonhole foot. Most buttonhole feet require you to place your button in a slot at the back in order to sew the correct-sized hole. Don't forget to pull the sensor lever down on your machine as well (this can vary between models so do check your machine manual if you are unsure) and select your desired buttonhole stitch.

4 Place a scrap piece of fabric under the presser foot and sew a practice buttonhole. If your machine sews a one-step buttonhole, it will complete the hole without any need for you to manipulate the fabric. Try not to pull the fabric in any way – let the machine do the work, and make sure to keep your hands out of the way of the sensor as this can cause the machine to misjudge the size of the hole. Check you are happy with the size and finish of your practice buttonhole, and if not, have another go – take as many practice runs as you need.

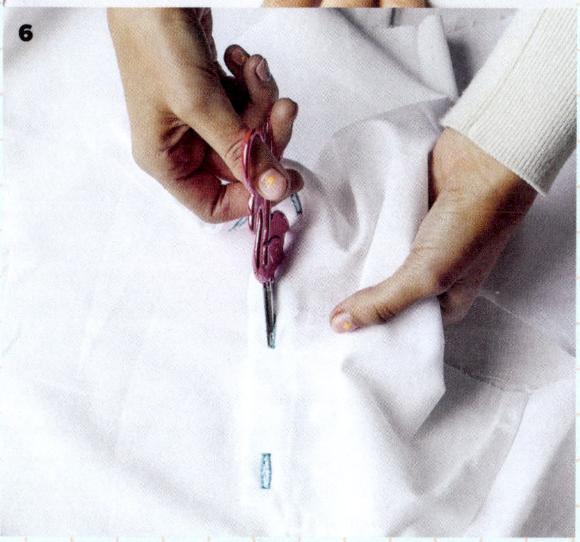

5 Once happy with the result, you can move on to the main garment. Line up the buttnhole marking or pin you placed earlier with the centre of the buttonhole foot and sew. Sewing slowly and in a controlled way will prevent any threads getting tangled. I will say that buttonholes on domestic sewing machines (particularly more basic models) are notorious for going haywire occasionally. If the buttonhole starts to go wrong, don't be afraid to stop sewing, turn your machine off and on again, and place the buttonhole foot back at the initial marking. It will sew over the previous stitches and hopefully continue as normal.

6 Take a sharp pair of thread snips, trim any loose threads and gently cut out the middle of the buttonhole to create space for your button. If you are nervous about cutting through the stitches, you can place a pin horizontally across the stitches at either end of the buttonhole to stop you from going through them.

7 To improve the longevity of your buttonholes, you may want to consider using a product such a Prym Fray Check or Hemline Fray Stopper. These liquid solutions are designed to be spread over the buttonhole threads and, once dry, will add some rigidity, preventing any fraying which can often happen over time.

Woo! Buttonholes complete! Now go and grab a cuppa, put on your favourite podcast (mine is true crime, always!) and enjoy sewing on those buttons as a finishing touch.

THE PARTY DRESS

A-line mini skirt, statement puff sleeves, heart cut-out

This design has to be one of my favourites and really does make the perfect dress for a special occasion. It's based on my 'hen-do' dress I made a few years ago, in which I had to mash up three different patterns to create what I had in my head. I just HAD to perfect the design and do all the hard work for you, so you could live out your ultimate occasion-dress dreams. Demure in the front, and party in the back – you'll be the belle of the ball in this one-of-a-kind mini dress.

Fabric suggestions

- Brocade/jacquard – why not try playing around with the reverse side of the fabric to create a contrast waist tie?
- Duchess satin
- Medium-weight cotton/broderie anglaise

Notions

- Sizes 6–14: 2.5m (2¾yd) of main fabric, 150cm (60in) wide. Sizes 16–22: 2.75m (3yd) of main fabric, 150cm (60in) wide
- Sizes 6–14: 0.5m (½yd) of lining fabric, 150cm (60in) wide. Sizes 16–22: 0.75m (1yd) of lining fabric, 150cm (60in) wide: I would highly recommend using the same fabric as for the dress so that if any of the lining shows around the heart cut out as you move in the dress, it isn't noticeable
- Iron-on woven interfacing of a similar weight to your chosen fabric
- Four hook-and-eye fastenings
- 1.2cm (½in) wide elastic

Notes

- All seams should be sewn with a 1cm (⅜in) seam allowance unless otherwise stated.
- Read through the technique tutorial on understitching (page 178) before you begin.
- Conversions to imperial measurements aren't always precise as they often need to be rounded up or down, but they do work with the patterns. Stick with either the metric or imperial measurements – don't mix and match.

Finished measurements

	6	8	10	12	14	16	18	20	22
Bust (cm)	96	101	106	111	116	121	126	131	136
Bust (in)	37¾	39¾	41¾	43¾	45½	47½	49½	51½	53½
Waist (cm)	56	61	66	71	76	81	86	91	96
Waist (in)	22	24	26	28	30	32	34	36	37¾
Front hem width (cm)	71.7	74.2	76.7	79.2	81.7	84.2	86.7	89.2	91.7
Front hem width (in)	28¼	29¼	30	31	32	33	34	35	36
Front length (cm)	90.8	91.4	92	92.6	93.2	93.8	94.4	95	95.6
Front length (in)	35¾	36	36¼	36½	36¾	37	37¼	37½	37¾
Sleeve length (cm)	35	35.5	36	36.5	37	37.5	38	38.5	39
Sleeve length (in)	13¾	14	14¼	14⅜	14½	14¾	15	15¼	15⅜

Elastic length

	6	8	10	12	14	16	18	20	22
Waist (cm)	57	62	67	72	77	82	87	92	97
Waist (in)	22½	24½	26½	28½	30½	32¼	34¼	36¼	38
Sleeve (cm)	24	25.6	27.2	28.8	30.4	32	33.6	35.2	36.8
Sleeve (in)	9½	10	10¾	11¼	12	12½	13¼	14	14½

Cutting guide

1 Bodice front – cut 1 on fold
2 Bodice front lining – cut 1 on fold
3 Bodice back – cut 2
4 Bodice back lining – cut 2
5 Bodice back interfacing – cut 2
6 Skirt front – cut 1 on fold
7 Skirt back – cut 1 on fold
8 Sleeve – cut 2
9 Waist tie – cut 2
10 Belt loop – cut 2

All sizes: 150cm (60in) wide main fabric

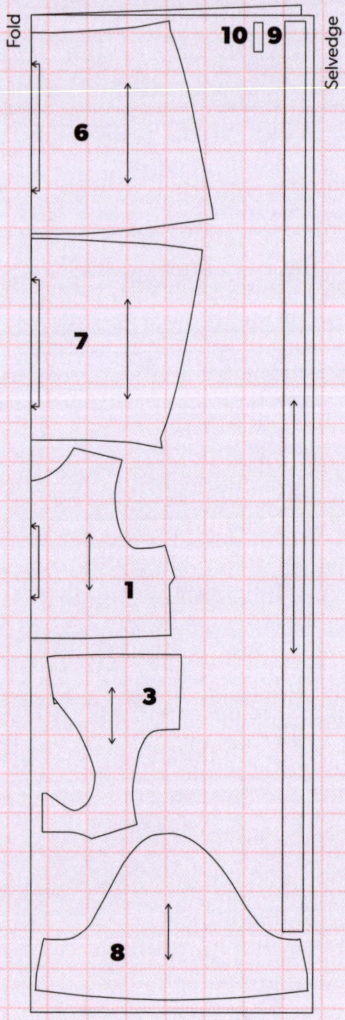

All sizes: 150cm (60in) wide lining fabric

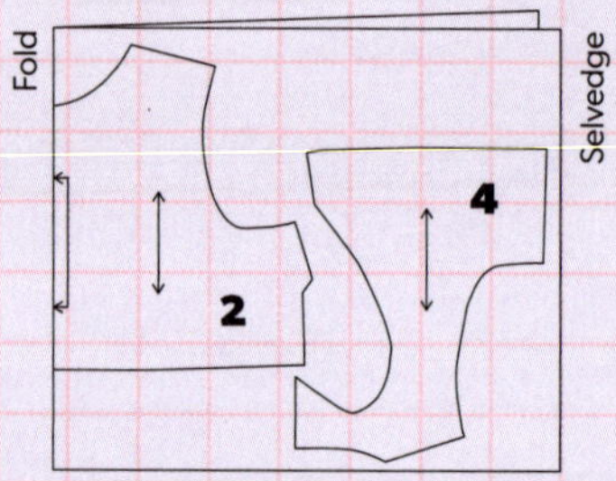

Interfacing

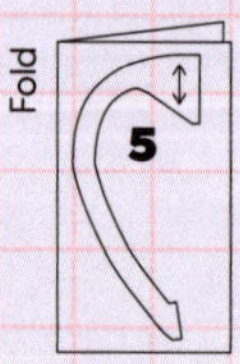

Pattern prep

1 Cut out all your pattern pieces from main fabric, lining and interfacing. Transfer all the notches and pattern markings, including darts.

2 Iron interfacing to the back-bodice pieces.

Preparing the main bodice

3 Stay stitch the neckline of the front bodice and lining to prevent any stretching of the fabric as you sew (see pages 19 and 83).

4 Using the markings you transferred from the pattern piece, sew the darts on the bodice front, leaving a long tail of thread to tie off at the end, and press the darts down towards the waistline.

5 With right sides together, sew the two bodice back pieces together at the centre back and press the seam open.

6 With right sides facing, pin the bodice front and back together at the shoulder and side seams. Stitch in place and press the seams open.

7 On the short end of each back bodice piece (where the hook-and-eye closures will be) press under 1cm (⅜in). This will create a fold that we will use to place our hooks and eyes. Hand-baste the hooks and eyes onto the fabric, lining them up with the pattern markings. The hooks should be on the right-hand side of the back bodice and the eyes on the left. Make sure the holes of the hooks and eyes are sat just within the seam allowance. (Beginners: feel free to skip this step and hand sew on the hooks and eyes to the inside lining once you have completed the dress.)

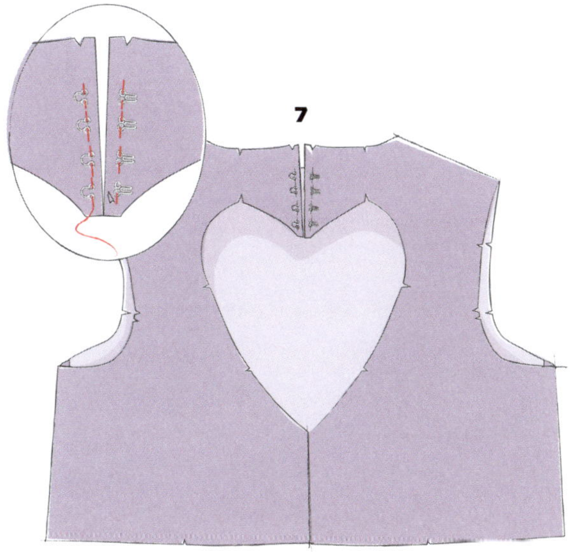

Preparing the lining

8 Sew the pleat in the front bodice lining by bringing the lower notch up to meet the second notch. Pin and baste in place at 0.5cm (¼in).

9 Sew the bodice back lining pieces together at the centre back and press the seam open, then sew the lining front and back at the shoulder and side seams as you did for the main bodice.

9

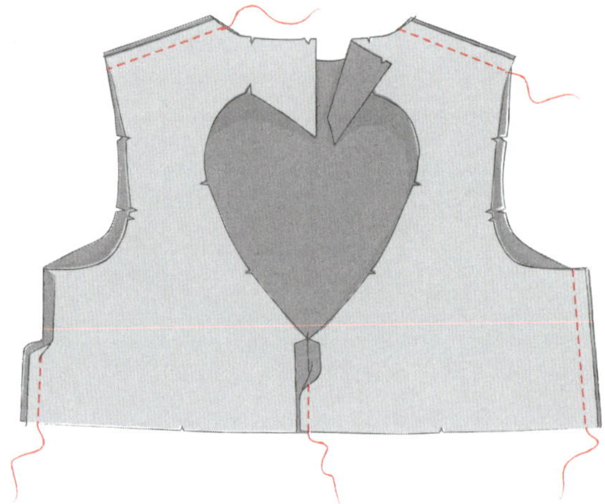

Attaching the lining to the main bodice

10 Place the main bodice inside the lining, right sides together. Start by pinning them together at the centre-front neckline and continue round to the shoulder seams and finally the heart back, making sure all the notches line up.

11 Once secure, stitch all the way round the neckline and heart cut-out, trying to avoid stretching out the fabric as you sew.

11

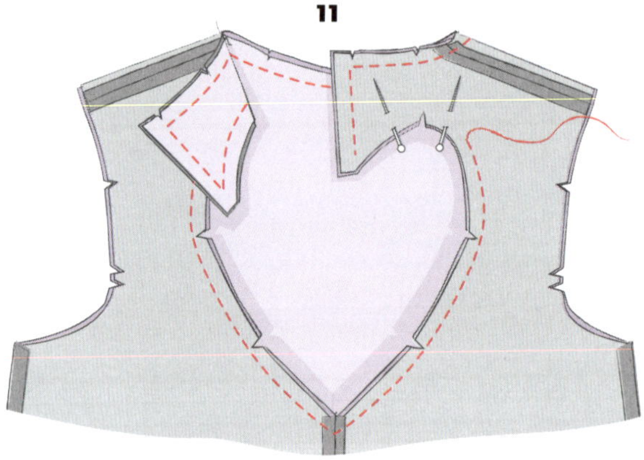

12 When you get to the short edge where we basted the hooks and eyes, switch to using the hand wheel on your machine to manually stitch over them. You may need to reduce your presser-foot pressure to do this.

13 Clip the corners and curved seam allowances, then understitch the seam allowance to the lining as far as possible at the front and around the cut-out (see my technique tutorial on understitching on page 178). Because of the deep curve of the heart, understitching will not be possible all the way round. Stop when you feel like the fabric is beginning to bunch up too much.

14 Turn the bodice right-side out with the lining sitting correctly underneath. You may need to use a chopstick or knitting needle to help push out the corners of the back closure.

15 Press well. This step is really important to ensure the bodice sits properly. Depending on the type of fabric you are using, you may wish to topstitch around the edge of the cut-out too.

Attaching the skirt

16 Finish the raw edges of the sides of the front and back skirt pieces using an overlocker (or zigzag).

17 Pin the skirt front and back right sides together at the side seams. Stitch in place with your standard 1cm (⅜in) seam allowance and press the seams open.

18 Matching the side seams and notches, pin the bodice to the skirt, with right sides facing, making sure the lining is out of the way. Sew this in place at 2.5cm (1in). Press this seam allowance up towards the bodice and then press under 1cm (⅜in) along the top of both layers of the seam allowance. This should leave you with a 1.5cm (⅝in) channel.

19 Before pinning the channel down, stroke the bodice lining down and tuck it behind the channel. The lining should be tucked behind the fold line by about 1cm (⅜in). Then pin the channel down on top of the lining, making sure it is completely flat and not pulling anywhere. This will hide all the raw edges and make a neat finish on the inside of your dress.

20 Now we can stitch the channel down, 0.2cm (⅛in) from the edge, making sure to leave a 2.5cm (1in) opening to insert the elastic.

21 Cut the length of waist elastic according to the size chart and, using a safety pin, gently feed this through the channel. This can sometimes be tricky with thicker fabric so take your time. Once fed through, stitch the ends of the elastic together before closing up the hole.

22 Gently stretch the waistline of the dress to adjust and even out the gathers.

18

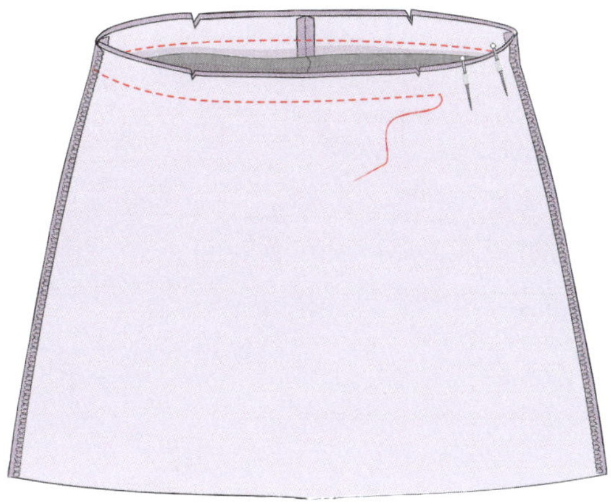

19

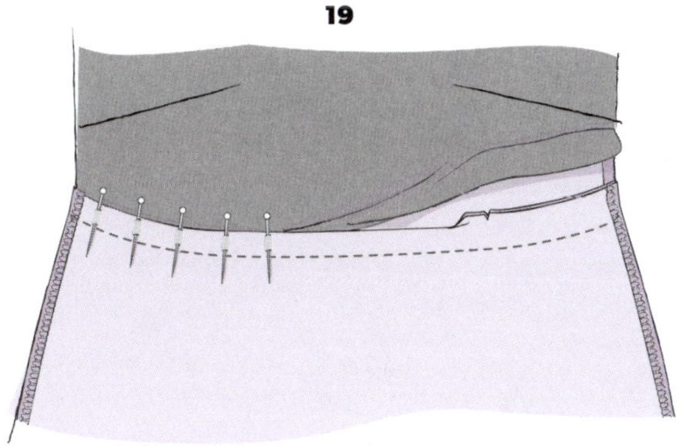

Top tip! I like to give my dress a good steam at this point to bring the elastic in if it has stretched out at all during the process.

Inserting the sleeves

23 Fold each sleeve right sides together to match the underarm edges and stitch the seam. Finish the raw edges as you wish.

24 Run two rows of gathering stitches between the notches on the sleeve head (see my technique tutorial on gathering on page 64). Make sure to leave a long tail of thread at each end.

25 Before inserting the sleeves, I like to prepare the elastic channel while the sleeves can sit fully flat, so press under 1cm (⅜in) all the way along the bottom edge of each sleeve, then press under another 3cm (1¼in) and pin in place.

26 Sew 1.5cm (⅝in) away from the outer edge and then edgestitch right along the pressed edge to create the elastic channel, once again leaving a gap of about 2.5cm (1in) to feed the elastic through. We will come back to this once the sleeves have been inserted.

27 Now, with right sides together, start by matching the underarm seams of the sleeves to the bodice armhole and pin them in place. Continue pinning all the way round to the gathering notches. The double notches should match with the bodice back. Then match the centre notches of the sleeve head and the armhole. You will now be able to see how much sleeve fabric you have to gather.

28 Gently pull on the gathering stitches until the fabric is the desired length. Evenly distribute the gathers and pin in place.

26

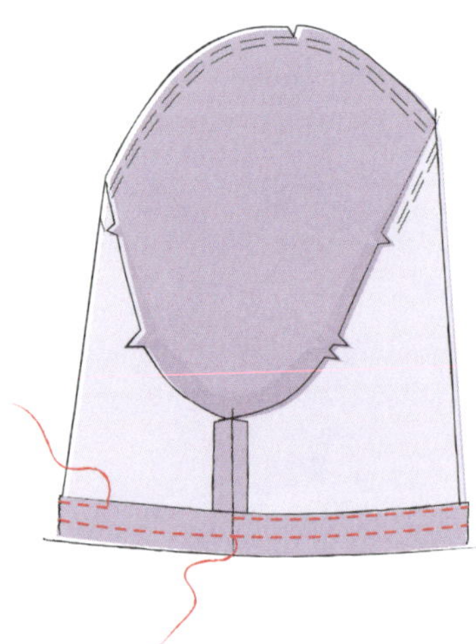

29 Stitch each sleeve into the armhole, being careful to keep the gathers even as you sew. Finish the raw edges. Check everything has been inserted correctly before unpicking any visible gathering stitches remaining and giving it a good press.

30 Cut the sleeve elastic according to the size chart and, using a safety pin, feed it through the channel we prepared earlier. Sew the short ends together and close up the hole.

Adding the belt

31 If you wish to add a belt to your dress, you'll want belt loops. Press your belt-loop pieces in half. Open out and press each raw edge to meet to the centre fold before pressing in half again (as when pressing binding). Edgestitch in place.

32 Press each short end of each belt loop under by 0.4cm (scant ¼in), and pin to the waistline of the dress following the pattern markings. Topstitch each of the short ends in place.

33 To prepare the belt, pin the belt pieces together with right sides facing. Starting from the middle of the belt, sew all the way round the edge, stopping 2.5cm (1in) away from where you started sewing. Clip the corners of the seam allowances and turn the belt out (you may need to use something pointed to fully press out the corners). At the opening, press under the remaining seam allowance and hand stitch this closed.

34 Heavy fabrics may need to be topstitched round the edge to keep the belt looking neat but pressing should be enough for light-/medium-weight fabrics.

33

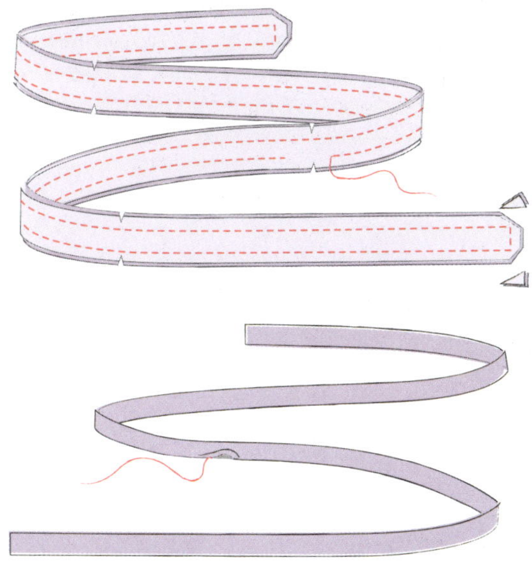

Finishing touches

35 Try on your dress to check you're happy with the length of the skirt, and shorten if needed. Overlock the hem edge and press under 2.5cm (1in) before stitching the hem in place.

Top tip! If you don't have an overlocker, you can create a double hem by first pressing under 1cm (⅜in) and then 1.5cm (⅝in) before stitching.

36 Give your dress a final press and trim any loose threads you may have.

Woo! Voila! You now have the perfect party dress – go show it off!

Styling suggestion

Don't be scared to layer up your party dress to get more wear out of it in the colder months! Try adding a plain turtleneck underneath and pairing it with tights and chunky black boots. You can still show off the heart cut-out feature without feeling the chill.

Technique Tutorial: *Understitching*

Understitching is an extra line of stitching we sew close to the edge to prevent a facing or lining from rolling to the front. It's particularly useful for neck facings or for lined garments, like our Party Dress, and will keep our heart cut-out looking crisp.

1 Sew the seam following the pattern instructions at, say, a neck edge.

2 Once stitched, press the seam allowances towards the facing or lining. If working on a curved seam, like our neckline or heart cut-out, you will need to clip into the seam allowances on the curves before pressing to keep them laying flat, taking care to cut as close as possible to the stitches without nicking any.

3 Now stitch the seam allowance down 0.2cm (⅛in) from the seam.

Top tip!

When it comes to understitching round sharp corners, it can be a bit tricky. If the fabric begins to bunch up, stop your stitches, leave a gap and then carry on stitching further round the bend. You don't need to stitch all the way along for the understitching to be effective.

4 Press the facing/lining to the inside of the garment. You will see that the row of understitching helps you to press the facing/lining evenly to the inside.

5 Stand back and admire your work! Your finished edge will look so much neater and more professional than if you hadn't understitched.

Woo! It really is as easy as that. A simple technique that will keep your garments looking professional!

STYLING PROJECTS

As 21st-century sewists, sustainability should be a key consideration in curating our handmade wardrobes. We should be saying goodbye to garments that only fit one occasion and hello to pieces that can be styled up no matter the weather. A capsule wardrobe will not only save you money, but also valuable time when putting outfits together. Unsure what this would look like in reality? Let me show you!

Spring

Summer

When the sun shines you can let the dress do the talking. Experiment with some frilly socks to keep your tootsies warm and dry in those April showers and play around with some accessories for extra interest.

Switch your headband for a sun hat to keep you cool on those hot summer days and pair it with a statement bag for another pop of colour.

Autumn

Just because this dress is figure hugging, doesn't mean it can't be layered up! Pair it with a pastel turtleneck for some extra warmth, and some trainers for a more wet-weather friendly option.

Winter

As temperatures really drop, style as a slip with a chunky knit and cosy scarf to keep you warm. Don't forget the hidden thermals for ultimate cosiness!

Spring

Summer

A cardigan is the perfect cosy but cute layering piece for this dress. Add a pearl bag and some satin shoes to keep it sweet!

No layering needed in the summer months, so show off those details and complement it with a cute headband to match! Ankle socks are a cool option but this would look equally good with some sandals.

Autumn

You can never have too many key colours, so double up with a turtleneck and knit in complementing colours. Skin-coloured tights are also a great option to cheat the bare-leg look when it's chilly.

Winter

Cold weather fashion doesn't have to be boring! Channel some Parisian chic with a beret and some pastel tights to complete a winter colour-block look.

RESOURCES

Fabric shopping can be quite the task for an inexperienced sewer, especially when you don't know where to start. To help beat the overwhelm, I've put together a list of my favourite places to shop, most of which can easily be found online. I also wanted to say a huge thank you to the businesses that have supplied fabrics and other materials that have helped this book come to life, and have marked those with an asterisk.

Alice Caroline Fabrics

www.alicecaroline.com

A fantastic supplier of Liberty fabrics.

Dalston Mill

www.dalstonmillfabrics.co.uk

A great source for affordable fabrics – perfect for wearable toiles!

Ebay

www.ebay.co.uk

Not to be overlooked as a great source of both haberdashery and fabrics for bargain prices.

Ethel & Joan

www.ethelandjoan.com

A small business specialising in hand-poured buttons in the most gorgeous colours.

Fabric Godmother*

www.fabricgodmother.co.uk

An excellent selection of high-quality dressmaking and dead stock fabrics.

Fabric Land

www.fabricland.co.uk

Another fantastic option to shop for a bargain. Buttons and other haberdashery are also available to buy in bulk at great prices.

Guthrie & Ghani*

www.guthrie-ghani.co.uk

A lovely independent shop with a range of dressmaking fabrics that you can also physically visit in Birmingham.

Hey Sew Sister

www.heysewsister.co.uk

One of my go-to places for on-trend cottons and viscoses.

Maison Fauve

www.maison-fauve.co.uk

High-quality and unique French fabrics – my favourite place to shops for jacquards and lace.

Minerva

www.minerva.com

A huge selection of all fabric bases – a great starting point for any project.

Rainbow Fabrics*

www.rainbowfabrics.co.uk

One of my favourites for ethically sourced dead stock fabrics in fun prints.

The Crafty Pie Shop

www.thecraftypieshop.com

Brogan's own brand of fabrics in collaboration with Visage Textiles. Head there for gorgeous ginghams and fun florals.

The Fabric Boutique

www.thefabricboutique.co.uk

A gorgeous shop local to me selling a range of dressmaking fabrics and patterns, both in-person and via their online shop.

INDEX

CREDITS

We have made every effort to contact and credit all the makers, artists and designers whose work appears incidentally in the book and will be more than happy to correct listings or add any omissions in future reprints.

Blue room

Swan cushion by Designers Guild

Stripe cushion by Oka

Ceramic vase by Romy Gordon

Pink room

Lampshade by Alice Palmer & Co

Wallpaper by Kit Kemp 'Mythical Lands' for Andrew Martin

Curtain fabric in 'Hester' (pink green) by Linwood

Library

White sculpture by Mabel Brim

Ceramic dish by Astier de Villatte

ABOUT THE AUTHOR

Brogan Allard is a sewer, social-media content creator and author based in Leicestershire. Formerly a secondary-school languages teacher, she has featured on Series 8 of the Great British Sewing Bee and now makes a whole host of content to inspire a new generation of 'stylish sewers'.

Alongside raising her young family, Brogan shares a variety of sewing inspiration through her highly successful social-media channels and offers fabrics and online workshops through her website www.thecraftypie.com. You can also find her blog on the website.

You can find Brogan here:
Instagram: @the_crafty_pie
TikTok: @the_crafty_pie
Website: www.thecraftypie.com

ACKNOWLEDGEMENTS

It seriously feels surreal to be writing the acknowledgements for my own book. In reality, I'm just a normal girl that's in love with sewing and has managed to build a community around her passion. This is such a 'pinch-me' moment that certainly couldn't have been achieved without the help of a lot of amazing people, so it's time to say a big thank you to them.

Firstly, I have to say a huge thank you to the amazing team at Quadrille, especially Ore and Emily. Thank you for believing in me and this book before I even dared to believe in myself. You've held my hand every step of the way and have made this experience an absolute joy.

To my amazing photographers Olivia and Elliya, my stylist Harriet, my makeup artists Cat and Danni and my editor Betsy, you truly brought my designs to life. Thank you for helping to fill these pages with pure dopamine.

To my husband Matt, thank you for keeping me nourished with tea and biscuits throughout the writing process, and for keeping me motivated through all those late-night sews. You never fail to be my biggest cheerleader and I couldn't do life (or a book!) without you.

And lastly to my gorgeous boy, thank you for showing me that I'm capable of anything. You are my sunshine and always will be.

Managing Director Sarah Lavelle

Editorial Director Harriet Butt

Project Editor Betsy Hosegood

Assistant Editor Oreolu Grillo

Art Director & Designer Emily Lapworth

Illustrator Robin Blair

Photographer Olivia Bossert and Elliya Cleveley

Stylist Harriet Langsbury

Hair & Make-up Cat Parnell and Danni Hooker

Models Brogan, Lucy and Pippa

Head of Production Stephen Lang

Production Controller Martina Georgieva

Published in 2024 by
Quadrille Publishing Limited

Quadrille
52–54 Southwark Street
London SE1 1UN
quadrille.com

 Cataloguing in Publication Data: a catalogue record for this book is available from the British Library.

ISBN 978 1 8378 3140 1

Printed in China

MIX
Paper | Supporting responsible forestry
FSC® C018179